EVERYTHING YOU TIRING BUT WERE AFRAID TO ASK. I have been working in accounting for over thirty years and did not know these things.
—STEPHEN BALLENGER
Accountant

This book really covers all the basics and it is very simple to read and understand. I recommend it to anyone looking for a place to start learning about investing. They say a journey of a thousand miles start with the first step. Let this be your first step to creation of wealth.
—RON BRUYN
Director, Orange County, California, Chapter of Better Investing

Where were you twenty years ago?!? I would hope this is read by everyone, especially woman 18–50 immediately! Your timing is perfect! Very succinct! Great analogies!
—JANE MORROW WRIGHT
Businesswoman

. . . .does a good job of presenting valuable information to the reader, especially to the beginning investor struggling to make sense of a complex subject.
—BILL SCHULTHEIS
Author of *The Coffeehouse Investor: How to Build Wealth, Ignore Wall Street and Get On With Your Life*

Janet's Holt's book really helped to explain finances to me in a basic manner that was readily comprehensible. It was also an eye-opener. I finally know for the first time ever, how much money I'll really need in order to retire! I highly recommend her book to others, especially women who are really interested in getting a handle on their finances.
—HELEN VERA, Ph.D.
Chair, Programs & Services for Women, San Antonio College

Janet Holt is a good writer with a style that makes for easy reading and quick comprehension. Her choice of words is excellent for beginning investors and she covers a lot of territory well.
—ELLIS TRAUB
Author of *Take Stock: A Roadmap to Profiting From Your First Walk Down Wall Street*

INVESTING
Starting from Scratch

Janet Holt

EAKIN PRESS Waco, Texas

Notice: The purpose of this book is to provide general information on investing. Neither the publisher nor the author are engaged in providing legal, financial or other professional services. Please seek the services of qualified professionals for legal or financial assistance and planning. The topics discussed in this book are meant to be examples and illustrations. It is recommended that you read other materials and learn as much as you can so you will be able to make informed decisions.

Every effort has been made to make the information in this book as accurate as possible, but be aware that changes in the financial world occur rapidly and there may be errors. The text should be used as a general guide for your edification.

If the above terms are unacceptable to you, you may return this book to your place of purchase or to the publisher for a full refund.

Intuit and QuickBooks are trademarks and service marks of Intuit Inc., registered in the United States and other countries.

Cartoons by Randy Glasbergen, used with his permission.

FIRST EDITION
Copyright © 2009
By Janet Holt
Published in the United States of America
By Eakin Press
A Division of Sunbelt Media, Inc.
P.O. Box 21235 ⌨ Waco, Texas 76702
email: sales@eakinpress.com
⌨ website: www.eakinpress.com ⌨
ALL RIGHTS RESERVED.
1 2 3 4 5 6 7 8 9
ISBN 978-1-934645-80-2
ISBN 1-934645-80-X
Library of Congress Control Number 2009924159

*Dedicated with affection to Robert Isbell,
who tried so hard to teach me this stuff.*

The Ant and the Grasshopper

In a field one summer's day, a grasshopper was hopping about, chirping and singing to its heart's content. An ant passed by, bearing along with great toil an ear of corn he was taking to the nest.

"Why not come and chat with me," said the grasshopper, "instead of toiling and moiling in that way?"

"I am helping to lay up food for the winter," said the ant, "and I recommend you do the same."

"Why bother about winter?" said the grasshopper. We've got plenty of food at present." But the ant went on its way and continued its toil. When winter came the grasshopper had no food and found itself dying of hunger, while every day it watched the ants distributing corn and grain from the stores they had collected in the summer. Then the grasshopper knew:

It is best to prepare for the days of necessity.

A Special Note:

When using personal pronouns, many writers alternate between he and she in an attempt to avoid sexism. As a reader, I find that confusing. Others use "he or she" or "his or her," but that is cumbersome. The fact is, we simply have not come up with a good inclusive pronoun yet. Although this book is appropriate for anyone who wants to learn about investing, I chose to use the feminine pronoun consistently in these pages. No offense, guys.

Acknowledgments

The financial professionals who generously provided their guidance and expertise to this project include Ralph Block, John Bogle, Richard Ferri, Scott Frush, Ray Lucia, Kathleen McKee, Stan Richelson, Bill Schultheis, Larry Swedroe, Ellis Traub and Ron Yolles. I am indebted to all of you.

The consultants and readers who helped shape the manuscript are Steve Ballenger, Ron Bruyn, Karen Cabral, Mike Castleberry, Michelle Columbo, Matt Cortese, Jon Gilland, Mary Helms, Kay Herring, Floyd Schultz, Linda Stillman, Jane Thielemann, Jill Torres, Linda Tyler, Helen Vera, Marilou Weir and Jane Wright. Thank you all for your comments, critiques and suggestions—you helped immeasurably.

To Kris Gholson, Pat Molenaar, Jim Tipton, and Kim Williams who made this book a book, you guys rock.

Special thanks to my husband, Mike, whose faith in me seems to be limitless.

And to Carla Burns who believed in this project from the beginning, thank you hardly seems adequate.

Contents

Foreword xiii
Preface: Learning the Hard Way. xv
Introduction: The Times They Are A-Changin'. xix

1. Starting from Scratch: Becoming a "Golden Egg" Farmer. . .   1
   - What Are Assets and Liabilities?
   - What Is Investing?
   - The Concept of Compounding
   - The Rule of 72
   - Asset Classes

2. Designing Your Henhouse 11
   - What Is a Portfolio?
   - Laying the Foundation
   - How Many Eggs Will You Need?
   - Counting Your Chicks Before They Hatch
   - Finding Your Number
   - Taking Inventory
   - Dreaming About What You Want
   - A Reality Check
   - Playing the Odds at Monte Carlo
   - How Long Do You Have to Gather Your Eggs?
   - What Kind of Hen Keeper Are You? Your Investing Style
   - Having Enough Baskets: Modern Portfolio Theory
   - Nailing It All Down

3. Buying Hens at the Stock Market 31
- What Is Stock?
- Learning Your Way Around The Market
- How Investors Make Money in The Stock Market
- Shopping Strategies
- Why Do Stock Prices Change?
- Why Are Stocks Split?
- What Kinds of Returns Can I Expect?
- How to Make a Purchase
- DIPS and DRIPS
- Other Animals in the Barnyard

4. Buying Hens at the Bond Market 47
- Bond Basics
- Types of Bonds
- Yields and Pricing
- More Bond Speak
- Effect of Interest Rates on Bonds
- Government Bonds
- Government Agency Bonds
- Corporate Bonds
- Making a Purchase
- Investment Strategies for Individual Bonds

5. Buying Hens at the Money Market 67
- Why Shop Here?
- What You Can Buy at the Money Market
- Making a Purchase

6. Buying Hens at the Real Estate Market................. 77
- What Are REITs?
- Learning Your Way Around the Market
- What You Can Buy at the Equity REIT Market
- How Investors Make Money with REITs
- Shopping Strategies
- Advantages of REITs Over Owning Individual Properties
- How to Make a Purchase
- Are REITs Good Investments?

7. The Mega Mart of Mutual Funds 91
   - What Is a Mutual Fund?
   - Learning Your Way Around the Market
   - To Manage or Not to Manage—That Is the Question
   - Exchange-Traded Funds
   - How Investors Make Money with Mutual Funds
   - Shopping Strategies
   - Other Considerations: Timing, Turnover and the Price of Fame
   - Consulting the Stars
   - Putting It All Together
   - Buying Funds

8. Browsing at the Specialty Market. 109
   - Hedge Funds
   - Buying on Margin
   - Short Selling
   - Derivatives
   - All That Glitters
   - Currency Trading
   - A Last Word of Caution

9. Guarding the Hens: Keeping the Fox out of Your Henhouse 127
   - Before You Make an Appointment
   - Assembling Your Financial Team
   - The Baskets
   - Who Will Hold Your Baskets?

10. Keeping Track of Egg Production. 139
    - What Kinds of Hens Do You Own?
    - How The Hens Are Laying: Measuring Returns
    - Tracking Tools
    - Maintaining Harmony in the Henhouse
    - Financial Housekeeping

11. Selling Your Eggs 149
    - Transitioning into Retirement
    - Selling Your Golden Eggs

- The RBD and The RMD for Your IRA According to the IRS
- Making Your Savings Last As Long As You Do with Annuities
- Reverse Mortgages
- A Final Word on the Subject

12. When You Don't Have Enough Eggs:
    A Plan for the Grasshoppers 163
    - Get Out of Debt
    - Dealing with Your Creditors
    - Don't Kill the Hens That Lay the Golden Eggs
    - Some Final Dos and Don'ts

13. Staying in Control of Expenses 177
    - Housing
    - Food
    - Transportation
    - Clothing
    - Everything Else
    - A Special Note for Those with Children
    - Work is Not a Four-Letter Word
    - A Reality Check

Epilogue: If It Is to Be. 189

Appendix I: Worksheets. 193
Appendix II: References and Resources. 198
Glossary 201
Citations. 211
Index. 213

Foreword

JANET HOLT IS A DYNAMIC and engaging writer who in these pages breaks down the walls that exist between the typical financial pro and everybody else. Janet explains her first look at this financial garble—and how it may as well have been written in ancient Sanskrit for how much sense it made to her. Instead of deciding that it was better left to the experts, Janet decided it was time to take control. She labored away to do research, asked questions, attended seminars and workshops and she became an expert herself. The result of her work is this enlightening book, *Investing Starting from Scratch*. Now, she can relay the information to those who are stressing to get to the truth about their money, who aren't in a position to spend literally hundreds of hours in research and study.

What Janet says is true, many financial gurus seem to speak their own language and what appears to be simple and obvious to them is neither. I have an extensive thirty-five-year background in the financial services industry. I realize that while all of this mumbo jumbo makes sense to me and my peers, the average American needs a basic guidebook to the slang and lingo that leaves most heads spinning. Americans need to improve their financial literacy and this book fills that need exceptionally. It explains money management and investment terms in a simple, easy-to-understand, and refreshingly useful way. Janet walks her readers through the world of mutual funds, investing, stocks, bonds and much more. Yes, it can be overwhelming, but Janet shows why this stuff is extremely relevant to our financial well-being, and therefore our lives. Janet's shared experience will help you learn from her mistakes, rather than making your own.

For the many Americans who feel lost in today's market and

don't know where to turn to combat the results the economy has had on their wallets, Janet provides an engaging walk through the ABCs of finance from someone who has real life experience learning it on her own. Everyone in America who is trying to figure this stuff out ought to pick up this book even before they read mine. My books, *Buckets of Money®: How to Retire in Comfort and Safety* and *Ready Set Retire! Financial Strategies for the Rest of Your Life* explain how to use my specific Buckets of Money® asset allocation strategy to ensure income and therefore financial stability at retirement. But my book, and most books that focus on strategy, starts somewhere in the middle. This book starts from scratch. It's step #1 financial planning, taking the reader through all of the basics without getting frustrated. If you know nothing about how to choose stock, what should be in your mutual funds, or what indexing means, then this book is for you. Janet will impart basic financial knowledge that will put you in control of your finances. She will share her wisdom and her personal experience. She will teach you and train you in the areas you need to know about before you invest dollar one. I highly recommend, *Investing Starting from Scratch*.

—RAY LUCIA

Preface

Learning the Hard Way

BEFORE YOU TURN ANOTHER PAGE, I want to tell you right up front that I am lousy at math. Numbers just don't speak to me the way they seem to do for some people. Oh, things started out well enough in school. The concept of "five apples take away three apples" made perfect sense—anyone could see you were left with two. Slice an apple down the middle and you get two halves—clear as day. The problem began with negative numbers. I simply could not understand how you could take anything away when you had nothing to start with. Later, when I was old enough to handle my own money, the meaning of less than zero became stunningly clear.

I also want to tell you that I have no background in finance, and I am not an investment advisor. In fact, before I learned what I'm going to share with you, I had lost nearly all my savings in the stock market. "So why," you may be asking yourself, "would I want to read this?" Because I am an expert on the subject of how *not* to invest your money. Contained in these pages is a synopsis of what I've learned the hard way to help you avoid my mistakes and start on your way to financial literacy.

My parents came of age in the Great Depression, so saving and preparing for a rainy day were predominant themes at our house. Like the dutiful ants, I faithfully contributed a portion of every paycheck to the retirement plan established by

> There is nothing like losing all you have in the world for teaching you what not to do. And when you know what not to do in order not to lose money, you begin to learn what to do in order to win.
> —EDWIN LEFEVRE

my employer. I was aware somebody, somewhere, did something with that money, but I didn't know who or what. I just assumed whoever it was knew a lot more about investing than I did. It all seemed so complicated. I tried reading the prospectuses provided by the brokerage firms, but they may as well have been written in ancient Sanskrit. When the financial report came on the nightly news, my eyes would glaze over. "Better to leave this to the experts," I would say as I went about the business of earning a living, confident my funds were in competent hands.

When I inherited some money, I was unprepared to make decisions about what to do with it. I found a wonderful financial advisor who tried so hard to make investing concepts clear, but my mind was snapped shut. Locked into the thinking that investing was too complicated to comprehend, I practically begged him to choose investments for me, which he reluctantly did. A little time passed, and then I made the first of two whopper mistakes. The market took a plunge. I panicked and sold "before it went any lower." This was despite the fact I really hadn't lost anything with the investments he had chosen for me.

As it has always done in the past, the market rallied (I missed out on this, of course, because I wasn't *in* the market) and I made mistake number two. I fell for the pitch of two salespeople who were—to put it delicately—less than scrupulous. They convinced me I needed to make up for lost time by making above average returns and they could make that happen. And indeed they did make above average returns—for themselves. They bought and sold with abandon and chose the mutual funds that paid them bonus commissions. I may not have known anything about investing, but I did know how to read the bottom line on those statements that arrived in my mailbox every quarter, and my balance was dwindling to a pittance. With very little left to lose, I finally decided it was time to take control.

I didn't have a clue what to do or how to do it. All I knew with certainty was I had to do *something* with what was left of my hard-earned cash, or watch inflation erode it away until it became a distant memory. I knew nothing about how to choose stock, or how to buy it even if I did know what I wanted. Indexing? What's that? REITs? Bonds? Zilch. No investing skills, no investing knowledge—nada. I turned to friends for advice. "How do you invest your money?" I would ask, to which they would reply, "I'm in mutual funds." "But what's in the mutual funds? Stocks? Bonds? A mixture?" I would persist. "I don't know," they would say with a tinge of annoyance, "they're just mutual funds." It quickly became apparent they were as clueless as I was and were going to be of no help in my investing education.

So I read. And read. And read some more. I would bring piles of books home from the library and prowl the shelves at bookstores. I attended workshops and seminars. I asked endless questions—and got a variety of different answers. The first thing I learned is that financial professionals speak their own language, and what seems simple and obvious to them is neither. I also learned there is no single "right" way to invest, no guaranteed formula—there are only guidelines and opinions. It is up to you and your trusted advisors to decide what mix and what method is the best for you. The old saying, "You pays your money and you takes your chances" is true, but the more you know, the better your odds of success.

I took copious notes to help me make sense of what I was reading and hearing—enough to fill a book. When friends began asking *me* questions about investing, I wanted to share my newfound knowledge with them—but in a simple, understandable way that wouldn't leave them as frustrated as I had been while researching. I decided to use an analogy, so I've built this book based on the adage, "Don't put all your eggs in one basket."

True to its name, this book starts with a look at the various types of golden eggs (assets) and their individual characteristics. I'll show you how to construct your henhouse (portfolio), then we'll visit the markets where the hens that lay the golden eggs are bought and sold. You'll learn to decipher the jargon in those glossy ads and prospectuses and how to choose your advisors and guardians carefully so you won't end up with a fox in your henhouse. We'll look at ways to keep track of your golden eggs and talk about portfolio management and the need to rearrange your mix from time to time as your flock grows. We'll talk about ways to sell your assets in a sustainable way, and how to ensure a steady supply of golden eggs. Investing terms that appear in italics can also be found in the glossary for quick reference later on. The book would not be complete without chapters for the grasshoppers among us. In the last two chapters you'll find practical suggestions for getting—and staying—out of debt, as well as ideas for finding soul-satisfying ways to produce income in your retirement years.

What you will *not* find in these pages is investment advice. There are already many good books and excellent advisors out there who can provide that for you. The only advice I will give you is this: learn all you can so you'll be able to make informed financial decisions. After all, who has more interest in your future well-being than you? So for all my fellow ants *and* grasshoppers out there starting from scratch, here is a summary written in simple terms of what I've learned the hard way. This is the book I wish I had found first. I hope it serves you well.

"First let me give you the good news... Your cat can still enjoy a comfortable retirement."

Introduction

The Times They Are A-Changin'

WE OFTEN SPEAK OF "traditional" retirement, but in the not-so-distant past, the concept of retirement was almost unknown. At the turn of the twentieth century, the United States was a largely agrarian society. Work on the farm was a family affair, and everyone was expected to contribute until they were no longer able. Life expectancy in 1900 was only about forty-seven years, so people worked, experienced a short period of illness or disability, and then they died. The "old" were respected and valued for their wisdom.

This picture began to change during the industrial revolution, as people migrated from farms to the cities. Factory jobs required speed, strength, and endurance—all characteristics of youth. Age, once revered, became a liability. The 1930s brought the Great Depression and the country sank into poverty—more than a quarter of the people in the United States were unemployed. The government, desperate to put people to work, found a solution. President Franklin Roosevelt officially institutionalized retirement when he signed the Social Security Act into law in 1935. This effectively removed those pesky older workers, and gave young workers a chance for the jobs they had vacated. Everybody was happy—except the retirees. Work was closely tied to feelings of self-worth, and provided a way for people to feel connected. Not surprisingly, many

> Otto von Bismarck, Chancellor of Germany, designed the world's first old-age social insurance program in 1889. This was largely a political gesture since he set the retirement age at seventy, but life expectancy in 1889 was only forty-eight.

people did not want to be put out to pasture and indeed, many did not live long enough to retire. Even though the mandated age for retirement was sixty-five, life expectancy in 1940 was sixty for men and sixty-five for women.

The early days of our retirement system were very different from the way it operates today. Benefit payments were designed to supplement personal savings and to keep retirees out of poverty—but just barely. These people were expected to use their few, final unemployed years for rest and reflection, and to get their affairs in order. The predominant view of retirement was a brief respite from a life of hard work before death. Pretty grim.

The Golden Years

And what happened to those younger workers? They had a bit of a rough start during the Depression, but then the end of World War II ushered in a period of peace and prosperity. The G.I. Bill provided a way for veterans to live the "American Dream." Low-cost loans enabled them to start businesses, pursue higher education, and own real estate. People bought homes, settled down, and for the most part, stayed put. Gender roles were clearly defined—men went to work and women stayed home to raise children and keep house. I recall a visit I had one afternoon with a ninety-year old acquaintance. While reminiscing about her early years, she told me there was only one employed woman on her block. She was such an oddity in the neighborhood that all the other women would gather at their windows to watch her leave for work in the morning. Her lifestyle provided a lot of fodder for coffee klatch gossip. How times have changed.

Men were "company men," often staying in the same job, or at least with the same employer, for their entire careers. Many companies provided pension plans to reward these loyal employees. By 1960, more than half the working population of the United States was covered by private pensions, and by 1980, the rate had jumped to eighty percent. During the 1950s, Social Security benefits increased by nearly eighty percent. Congress authorized automatic cost-of-living increases to pensioners and introduced Medicare in 1965—life was good.

As poverty rates among the elderly plummeted, the concept of retirement changed from one of a few years of poverty and declining health to the "Golden Years." Life expectancy had increased dramatically, and people began retiring younger and healthier. The Golden Years were viewed as a time to escape responsibilities and enjoy a carefree life filled with play, funded by newfound wealth. The ideal retirement was eagerly anticipated as one long vacation, and the earlier one could get started, the better.

The Retirement Revolution

All these prosperous, settled people produced the huge number of children known as the "Baby Boomers." Born between 1946 and 1964, this generation has had enormous influence over every stage of their lives—and retirement will be no exception. Boomers came of age in an era of discovery, technological advances, and tremendous cultural change. They are more likely to have higher educations and to seek personal meaning in their work. This desire, along with high mobility, has made job and career changes the norm rather than the exception. Medical breakthroughs coupled with healthier lifestyles have created a generation that can expect to be energetic and productive well into their eighties and beyond.

This generation is not inclined to "go gentle into that good night" (Dylan Thomas), and even less likely to engage in a lifestyle of endless leisure. Survey after survey indicates as many as eighty-five percent of Boomers plan to continue working—at least part-time—well past the traditional retirement age. Some will work because many of us took "live for today" a little too literally and have failed to save enough money to retire. Others see it as a time to pursue new interests, fulfill dreams, and follow their bliss; the trend is toward starting over rather than wrapping up. Whatever the motivation, Baby Boomers are redefining the concept of retirement and going boldly where no one has gone before. It should be quite a ride.

> Sha-la-la-la-la-la, live for today
> And don't worry 'bout tomorrow, hey, hey, hey
> —Written by Doc Pomus and Mort Shuman, recorded by the Grass Roots

What You Don't Know Can Hurt You

The days when a company could expect a worker to sign on for twenty plus years, and when a worker could reasonably expect the company to take care of her after retiring are over. Loyalty? What's that? There has been a dramatic shift in recent years from *defined benefit plans* (traditional pensions) to *defined contribution plans* (like 401(k)s and 403(b)s). Talk about privatizing or making other changes to Social Security continues. "Outsourcing" and "downsizing" (a polite word for "firing") are facts of modern life, and older workers are often the first to go. Okay, so you've got a 401(k) that will go with you. Do you know who is managing the fund and what it's invested in? Does it matter? Ask the displaced workers from Enron that question.

There is just no way around the fact that *we* are responsible for our own financial futures. Even if you have someone in your life who takes care of financial planning for you, you should at least be able to read and understand your investment account statements. Failing to have a basic understanding of investing is setting yourself up for potential disaster. A 2007 survey conducted by the Employee Benefit Research Institute reported that almost a quarter of the workers interviewed were unaware that they don't even have a pension plan at work. Can you imagine their shock when they're ready to retire? Other studies reveal between thirty and forty percent of American workers age forty and older have no retirement savings. Remember the poor old grasshopper that starved to death because of his failure to prepare for the winter? Of course, he didn't have Social Security to fall back on. And speaking of that...

Do You Really Want to Depend on Social Security?

Many people have the mistaken idea that the contributions they have made to Social Security through payroll deductions go into some sort of account, earmarked for their retirement years. In reality, Social Security is a pay-as-you-go system. That means the payroll taxes withheld from your check are providing benefits for current retirees. As long as there are many workers to support the retirees, the burden is easy to bear. The predicted crunch will come because the

Boomers produced fewer children and are living longer than ever before, so fewer workers will be supporting a huge number of retirees for what could be a very long time. In 1950, the ratio of workers to retirees was sixteen to one. As of this writing (2008), the ratio of workers to retirees is about three to one and declining.

Of course, projections on the future of Social Security vary depending upon which politician is pontificating on the issue. A solution to current problems may well be found but even so, Social Security was never designed to be a pension plan. It was designed to act as a safety net to keep people out of poverty while they depended primarily on their own savings. Do you really want to depend on Social Security as your sole source of income?

Why Financial Knowledge Is Essential for Women

Women have a high risk of finding themselves alone in their later years. There are a number of reasons for this:

- Divorce has become a fact of modern life, and the odds of a woman remarrying after age fifty are not in her favor.
- As employment opportunities have expanded, the number of women who never marry is increasing.
- Women live longer than men in almost every nation in the world. Although the gap is closing somewhat, the average in the United States is still about five years longer.
- Women have a tendency to marry older men, which can significantly increase the number of years spent solo.
- The U.S. Census Bureau pegs the average age of widowhood in this country at fifty-six. If you have any doubts that old women outnumber old men, visit any senior center or nursing home.

More and more women have entered the workforce, but it is still a sad fact they have lower lifetime earnings than men. Women still earn only about seventy percent of what men do, and are more likely to work part-time or take time off from work to raise children and/or care for elderly parents. This means that women are much less likely to be covered by private pensions than men who have uninterrupted careers. There is still more bad news. The pension wealth of a single woman vested in a private pension plan averages only thirty-four percent of the pension wealth of a single man. Women over sixty-five have double the poverty rate of men the same age, and make up almost three-quarters of older Americans who must exist on poverty level incomes. Enough statistics—you get the picture.

It is not difficult to find stories about elderly people who are victims of scams and unscrupulous "advisors." I don't want to be one of those victims and I don't want you to be, either. Now, ask yourself one question, *"If I don't take charge, who will?"* Are you ready? Excellent! Let's get started.

> **An investment in knowledge always pays the best interest.**
> —BENJAMIN FRANKLIN

"People are afraid of bears and bulls! From now on, our brokerage will use bunnies and kittens."

CHAPTER ONE

Starting from Scratch: Becoming a Golden Egg Farmer

W̲E ALL KNOW THE ADAGE, "Don't put all your eggs in one basket." But exactly what are these golden eggs? And how do you get them? This is where we will begin.

What Are Assets and Liabilities?

An *asset* is simply an item of economic value; something you own. Our goal as investors is to gather a sufficient number of assets or golden eggs to achieve a degree of financial independence in our later years. Like all good endeavors, you need to have a plan for how to accomplish this goal. A good place to start is by determining how many eggs you already have, or your *net worth*.

Begin by making a list of everything you own, taking into account both financial and non-financial assets. Use Worksheet 1 in Appendix I to help you. Financial assets include the current balances in your bank and savings accounts, the cash in your wallet, and the change you have accumulated in those coffee cans. Also include the value of any stocks, mutual funds, or bonds you may own, as well as the current balances of retirement and investment accounts such as IRAs, 401(k)s and 403(b)s. If you have life insurance with cash value, include that amount. If you haven't ever opened your statements, now would be a good time.

Non-financial assets are tangible things like real estate, fine art, jewelry, antiques, collections —coins or stamps, for example—automobiles, and anything else of value that could be sold. These assets have value based on their individual properties. Some *appreciate* (or increase) in value over time; others *depreciate* (or lose value). Real estate is an example of an appreciating asset. Usually, but not always, the value of a property *increases* over time—this is why home ownership may be desirable. As you pay down your mortgage, the amount you have invested in your home increases. The difference between the market value of your home and the amount you owe a lender is your *equity*, or what you would get to keep if you sold it. The key is to take good care of real estate and hold on to it over the years, hoping no one builds a nuclear reactor nearby in the meantime. Your car, on the other hand, is an example of a depreciating asset. The longer you own it, the less it's worth. Depreciation of a new car begins the minute you drive it off the dealer's lot. If you decide to sell it after a few years, it will fetch only a fraction of its original price. Of course, keep it long enough for it to become an antique, and the market value could go up again—nothing in life is absolute.

After you finish your list of assets, which we'll call List A, you're ready to move on to liabilities. A *liability* is a debt; something you owe. Make another list of anything you owe—such as the balances of your mortgage, car note(s), student loans, credit cards, and any other outstanding loans. We'll call this List B. All that's left to do is subtract List B (what you owe) from List A (what you own), and the result is your net worth (your eggs). Now you know your starting point. If the total of List B is greater than the total of List A, you have less than zero eggs, so your first step is to get out of debt. You'll find some ideas to help you do that in Chapter Twelve, and the sooner the better. Please don't waste time berating yourself about it, because you have lots of company in our must-have-it-now society. Just resolve to do things differently from now on, and get started with a payment plan.

What Is Investing?

You want more golden eggs, but how do you get them? One of the best ways is by putting your money to work for you. *Investing* simply means putting *capital* (cash) into something (such as securities) with the expectation of making a return. A *security* is an instrument representing ownership that has value and can be bought and sold. Although there are numerous financial products on the market, there are only two general ways to make money from investing: owning or loaning.

- **Equity ("ownership") investments.** Something is bought, improved upon or held until it increases in value, and then sold for a profit. Examples of this type of investment are real estate or stocks. Stocks, then, are equity securities.
- **Debt ("loanership") investments.** Income comes from interest payments on money you have loaned. When you purchase a certificate of deposit, for example, you have actually loaned money to the bank. The bank pays interest to you, then uses your money to make loans to others—at a higher interest rate, of course. Bonds are another example of this type of investment. Bonds are debt securities.

The Concept of Compounding

When asked what he considered mankind's greatest invention, Albert Einstein is reported to have said "compound interest." Some sources quote him as calling it "the greatest mathematical discovery of all time." Other sources are not sure he actually said anything about it at all, but whether he did or didn't, there is solid truth in the concept. Let's look at simple interest first.

Simple interest is the money earned only on your *principal* or initial investment. Here is an example: Ima Investor has $1,000 she wants to invest. She sees her bank is selling thirty-six month certificates of deposit (CDs) at an *annual percentage rate* or APR of ten percent. (I realize ten percent may be unrealistic depending on market conditions, but it is an easy number to work with for our examples.) This means the term or length of time until the CD matures is three years, and it pays ten percent simple interest each year. Ima calculates her future earnings using this formula:

Principal × Interest Rate × Term
OR
$1,000 × 10% × 3 Years

INVESTING STARTING FROM SCRATCH

Each year, the CD will earn $100, so at maturity it will be worth $1,300. Simple, right?

Now let's look at *compound interest*, which earns interest on the principal (initial investment) *and* on the reinvested earnings. Compounding periods vary, but will usually be annually, semi-annually, quarterly, or monthly. Here is an example of how it works: If Ima is considering a CD earning interest that is compounded annually, the first year it will earn $100, the same as our simple interest note. The formula for calculating this is:

$$\text{Principal} \times \text{Interest Rate} \times \text{\# of Compounding Periods}$$
OR
$$\$1,000 \times 10\% \times 1 \text{ Year}$$

Here is where things get interesting. The $100 earned is added to the principal for a new total of $1,100. At the end of year two, the interest would be $110:

$$\$1,100 \times 10\% \times 1 \text{ Year}$$

That $110 is added to the principal for a new total investment of $1,210. At the end of the third year, the interest would be $121:

$$\$1,210 \times 10\% \times 1 \text{ Year}$$

Ima finds the value of the CD at maturity would be $1,331:

Initial investment:	$1,000
+ Year 1 interest:	100
+ Year 2 interest:	110
+ Year 3 interest:	121
Total	$1,331

You can see each year the principal amount would increase, so she would earn interest on a higher amount—interest is earning interest on interest. "Big deal," you may be thinking, "thirty-one dollars more." You're right, it's not much. But what if the interest were compounded quarterly instead of annually? The difference between the simple interest return and the compounded return would be almost $345. Does this look a little more interesting?

Starting from Scratch: Becoming a Golden Egg Farmer

The longer you hold your investment, the more you will earn as it accumulates (or compounds). Like a snowball going downhill, it picks up speed as the years roll along. Here is a vivid example. If I gave you the choice of taking $300,000 cold cash right now or a single penny doubled every day for the next thirty days, which would you take? If you chose the lump sum, you would have lost earnings of more than $5 million! (*Fig. 1*). I know it sounds preposterous, but if you're skeptical, get out your calculator and see for yourself. Now it's easy to see why Einstein was so impressed.

> **A penny saved is a penny earned.**
> —BENJAMIN FRANKLIN

Power of Compounding			
Day 1	$0.01	Day 16	$327.68
Day 2	$0.02	Day 17	$655.36
Day 3	$0.04	Day 18	$1,310.72
Day 4	$0.08	Day 19	$2,621.44
Day 5	$0.16	Day 20	$5,242.88
Day 6	$0.32	Day 21	$10,485.76
Day 7	$0.64	Day 22	$20,971.52
Day 8	$1.28	Day 23	$41,943.04
Day 9	$2.56	Day 24	$83,886.08
Day 10	$5.12	Day 25	$167,772.16
Day 11	$10.24	Day 26	$335,544.32
Day 12	$20.48	Day 27	$671,088.64
Day 13	$40.96	Day 28	$1,342,177.28
Day 14	$81.92	Day 29	$2,684,354.56
Day 15	$163.84	Day 30	**$5,368,709.12**

Fig. 1

The Rule of 72

Alas, as lovely as that sounds, investments in the real world do not double daily. But there is a handy little trick to figure out how long it will take to double your money when it compounds at a particular rate of annual interest called the *Rule of 72*. All you have to do is divide seventy-two by the rate of interest you are getting, and the result is the number of years it will take to double your money. For example, Ima's CD was at a compounded interest rate of ten percent. If she wanted to know how long she would have to hold the note before she doubled her money, she would divide seventy-two by ten. She would find she'd have to hold the note for 7.2 years.

Asset Classes

Different types of investments are categorized into groups known as *asset classes*. The big four are stocks, bonds, cash, and real estate. We will discuss them all in more detail in subsequent chapters, but here is a general overview:

Stocks aka Equities

I used to say that buying stock is like going to Las Vegas and putting money on the roulette table—but I was wrong. Buying stock is actually becoming part owner of a company, hence the name "shares" of stock.

As noted earlier, stocks are ownership investments. When a company needs additional money to pay for growth, the managers have two choices. They can borrow it, or if they don't wish to incur debt, they can raise money by selling part ownership in the company. They do this by issuing stock. Just as a business has no guarantee of success, the shareholder is not guaranteed a return. Because of the increased risk associated with buying stock, returns are generally higher than with other types of investments.

Historically, the stock market has outperformed everything else over time. Why? Because our world economy is based on production and growth, and that means growth of companies. If you look at all the graphs—which you can find in abundance online and in financial publications—you will see a zig-zagged but generally upward-moving line indicating that stock market growth has plenty of down periods. When market prices are generally headed downward, it's called a *bear market*. *Bull markets* are periods of optimism, when the market begins a rally and sustains upward movement after being at or near the bottom. Up and down it goes, but over long periods it has gone up more than it has gone down, so it's easy to see why *over time* are the

Starting from Scratch: Becoming a Golden Egg Farmer

operative words in the first sentence of this paragraph. Investing in stock is not risk-free, but if you do your homework, you can greatly improve your odds of success. The key to protecting yourself in the stock market is to understand not only where you put your money but *why*. Peter Lynch, a hugely successful mutual fund manager, has been quoted as saying, "Never invest in any idea you can't illustrate with a crayon." Critics say this is oversimplified, but I say, the simpler, the better.

Bonds

When our government spends more than it collects through taxes, it must borrow to finance the deficit. If a company wishes to raise money without issuing stock, they also must borrow it. The government and large companies need huge sums of money—more than they can borrow long-term from banks. To get it, they go to the public market where they find investors who each lend a portion of what is needed in exchange for a bond. Bonds are nothing more than loans made to an entity—government or corporate—for a pre-determined length of time at a pre-determined rate of interest—in other words, glorified IOUs or *debt instruments*. Depending on bond quality, there may be less risk in owning bonds than in owning stocks, but the return is generally lower. In the event of a bankruptcy, bondholders' claims on assets (if there are any left) come before stockholders. Bonds are known as *fixed income investments* because you know in advance the exact amount you will receive for them if you hold them until their maturity. Bonds add diversity to your portfolio, help reduce volatility, and provide a stable, reliable source of income.

Cash

When the big players need to borrow cash for short periods, they are likely to turn to the money market. Like bonds, money market instruments are basically IOUs issued by the government, banks, and large corporations, but usually for terms of less than one year—some are as short as one day. These fixed-income investments offer returns to investors in the form of interest payments. Offerings in the money market are considered extremely safe, meaning significantly lower returns.

You will often hear money market investments referred to as "cash investments." The most common are certificates of deposit (CDs) and Treasury bills (or T-bills). These instruments are popular because they are widely available, uncomplicated, and can be purchased with small sums. CDs and T-bills can be purchased directly. Other products, such as commercial paper and banker's acceptance notes, require huge sums of money to buy, so most individuals invest in these through mutual funds.

A Word About Inflation

Inflation is the rate at which prices are rising. Can you remember what a movie ticket cost when you were a kid? A burger and a Coke? A look at prices for these same items today paints a clear picture of the effects of inflation. *Inflation risk* is the risk that all your gains will be gobbled up while you wait for your debt securities to mature, leaving you with nothing more—or in a worse case scenario—less than you started with. Debt securities with longer terms usually offer higher interest rates to help offset this risk since no one can be certain what future inflation rates will be.

> A nickel ain't worth a dime anymore.
> —YOGI BERRA

The handy Rule of 72 can also be used to calculate the number of years it will take for the buying power of your money to be cut in half by inflation. For example, if we assume an average inflation rate of three percent, we can determine your money will be worth half what it is today in about twenty-four years (72 divided by 3).

Real Estate (Can be Ownership or Loanership Investment)

You have no doubt heard it said that your home is your most important investment—but is that true? The answer is—it depends. It depends on such things as where you live, how long you own your house and what condition the property is in. Let's look at some of the variables.

First of all, the only way to recognize the gain on your investment is to sell your home. If you live in a desirable area, *all* the housing values have gone up as much as yours has. That's great for selling prices, but once you've sold, you have to find somewhere else to live. Unless you downsize or relocate to where the cost of living is much lower, you'll have to reinvest the proceeds in a new abode—so much for your gains. If your area has become less than desirable due to such things as major industry openings or closings, it may be worth less than you'd hoped—sometimes much less. Times of economic crisis can also negatively affect the value of your home—hopefully temporarily. Property taxes, insurance, maintenance costs and selling expenses can take a big bite out of your budget, and people who must sell their homes quickly often find themselves in precarious positions. I'm not trying to discourage anyone from home ownership; just cautioning you to be realistic in assessing its value as an investment. Also, remember you can only count your equity as an asset—the rest of the eggs belong to the lender.

Of course, you can buy real estate to resell or to use for rentals if you are so inclined. Many fortunes have been made in real estate and there are hundreds of books on that subject, too. But if the idea of being a "rehabber" or a landlord doesn't excite you, there is a less cumbersome way to invest in properties. Real Estate Investment Trusts, or REITs as they are commonly known, are direct investments in real estate that sell like stock on the open market. Investors participate in income produced through rents, leases, and property sales. REITs are required by law to distribute nearly ninety percent of their taxable annual income to their shareholders, making them popular with investors looking for income.

THE BOTTOM LINE

- Assets are things you own. They can be financial, such as cash or bonds, or non-financial, such as real estate, antiques or jewelry.
- Liabilities are what you owe.
- The difference between assets and liabilities is your net worth.
- Investing means putting your money to work for you.
- There are two basic types of investments: equity (ownership) and debt (loanership).
- Albert Einstein reportedly called compounding "the greatest mathematical discovery of all time."
- The Rule of 72 allows an investor to determine how long it will take to double money at a particular rate of interest.
- Investments are divided into asset classes. The major ones are stocks, bonds, cash, and real estate.
- There is a correlation between risk and return: The greater the risk, the greater the potential return. (*Potential* is the operative word).
- Each type of investment has its own risks and rewards. Deciding which is best for you depends on your goals, time frame, and tolerance for risk.

CHAPTER TWO

Designing Your Henhouse

What Is a Portfolio?

IN THE NOT-SO-DISTANT PAST before everything was computerized, investors received paper certificates of ownership when they purchased stock. These stock certificates required safekeeping, so wealthy people often kept them in safe deposit boxes at their banks. When they had accumulated enough of them to fill an expanding folder, they referred to it as their *portfolio*. Things are different today. Stock ownership is usually recorded electronically, and the term "portfolio" is used to describe your total savings and investments—all the golden eggs you have managed to accumulate. How do you get more of these eggs? You buy some golden hens, of course. We will visit the markets in the next chapters, but first you need to decide what types of hens you want and how many you need. It's time to design your henhouse.

> Noah started building the ark BEFORE it began to rain.
> —NORMAN R. AUGUSTINE

Laying the Foundation

We all want to gather enough eggs to achieve a level of financial independence when we retire. How many is that? Who can tell you? Every financial guru you hear, screaming (sometimes literally) for your attention, seems to have a different answer, and all those ads for brokerages and financial services can leave you feeling more confused than ever. Having too many choices leads to inertia, so you put off creating a plan a little longer. How can anybody be expected to plan amidst all the noise? Like Scarlett O'Hara, you resolve to think about it tomorrow.

The reality is there is no single answer for every situation. How many eggs it will take to meet your needs depends on your lifestyle and your dreams. I know people who could make a million dollars a year (or more) and still not be satisfied, and I know others who live quite happily on a tiny fraction of that amount. Author Lee Eisenberg calls your target net worth your "number" in his book, *The Number: A Completely Different Way to Think About the Rest of Your Life*. Finding your very own number is what this chapter is about.

> My definition of a guru is someone who is lucky enough to be quoted in the right publication at the right time saying the right thing.
> —HERB GREENBERG

How Many Eggs Will You Need?

Since we are on the subject of numbers, it's time to crunch a few of them so you can estimate how much income you will need when you're ready to quit working. It doesn't matter how far in the future it might be, you'll be using today's dollars for this exercise. Relax—this doesn't involve advanced mathematics—just a bit of research, an ordinary calculator, and three simple worksheets. You'll find the blank worksheets you need in Appendix I in an easy-to-copy format and you'll have a guide, Ima Investor, to help you. You met her briefly in the last chapter, so let's learn a little more about her now. Ima is forty years old and divorced with no children. She lives and works in Dallas, Texas, earning $48,500 per year. Five years ago, she took out a $108,000 mortgage on a townhouse currently valued at $136,500. Ima will create her worksheets along with you so you can see how the process works.

The first step is to determine your current annual expenses. Do you know where your money goes? If not, it's time to find out. Go through your bank statements or check registers and add up your routine monthly expenses. You don't have to examine an entire year's worth of statements, but do enough to get an accurate picture of an annual total. Use your pay stubs for tax amounts

Designing Your Henhouse

and any insurance premiums that may be deducted from your paycheck. Don't forget to add in any non-routine expenses you may have, such as insurance premiums paid quarterly or taxes paid annually. You can use Worksheet 2 in Appendix I to help you with this task. When you've finished you will have established a starting point from which to work. Ima's completed Worksheet 2 is shown in Fig. 2.

> All the flowers of all the tomorrows are in the seeds of today.
> —Indian proverb

Fig. 2: Ima Investor's Worksheet

Worksheet 2: Annual Expenses		
Housing	Monthly	Yearly
Mortgage or rent	$ 630.26	$ 7,563.12
Electricity	180.00	2,160.00
Gas	0.00	0.00
Water	30.00	360.00
Repairs & Maint.	20.83	250.00
Other		
Subtotal	861.09	10,333.12
Transportation		
Car payment	310.00	3, 720.00
Fares	0.00	0.00
Fuel	120.00	1,440.00
Repairs	14.58	175.00
Other	6.83	82.00
Subtotal	451.42	5,417.00
		(continued next page)

Worksheet 2: Annual Expenses *(continued)*

Insurance	Monthly	Yearly
Homeowners	$ 99.00	$ 1,188.00
Auto	47.00	564.00
Health	143.57	1,722.84
Life	0.00	0.00
Other		
Subtotal		
Food		
Groceries	280.00	3,360.00
Dining out	75.00	900.00
Other		
Subtotal	355.00	4,260.00
Personal		
Medical	25.00	300.00
Clothes	40.00	480.00
Laundry	8.00	96.00
Memberships	18.00	216.00
Haircuts/Personal	20.83	250.00
Other		
Subtotal	111.83	1,342.00
Entertainment		
Movies/Videos	20.00	240.00
Cable	49.00	588.00
Concerts/Events	0.00	0.00
Books/Music	19.00	228.00
Other		
Subtotal	88.00	1,056.00

(continued next page)

Worksheet 2: Annual Expenses *(continued)*

Loans	Monthly	Yearly
Student	$ 0.00	$ 0.00
Credit card	68.00	816.00
Other		
Subtotal	68.00	816.00
Taxes		
Federal	1,054.00	12,648.00
State	0.00	0.00
Local	0.00	0.00
Property	181.42	2,177.00
Subtotal	1,235.42	14,825.00
Gifts		
Friends/Family	30.00	360.00
Charity	10.00	120.00
Other	5.00	60.00
Subtotal	45.00	540.00
Professional		
Dues	15.00	180.00
Attorney	0.00	0.00
Other (C.P.A.)	16.67	200.00
Subtotal	31.67	380.00
Savings		
Retirement	405.00	4,860.00
Investment	100.00	1,200.00
Other		
Subtotal	505.00	6,060.00
Totals	**$4,042.00**	**$48,503.96**

Now, visualize yourself in the future and imagine you are already retired. How have things changed? Do you still have a mortgage? How about other debts? Are you still paying professional dues? Have your health care expenses increased? Consider the changes you expect to take place and make the necessary adjustments to your figures. You will want to deduct payroll taxes and any contributions you now make to retirement or investment accounts since you will no longer make these when you are not working. It doesn't have to be to the penny—your best estimate will suffice. Stick to basic expenses for this exercise and when you've finished, you will have an idea of the amount of income you will require later to maintain your current standard of living. Enter that amount in Column A on the worksheet entitled "Finding Your Number" (Worksheet 4).

Ima finishes gathering her figures and estimates she will need $42,500 each year to fund her basic needs. Ima earns $48,500 now, but thinks she can live on less when she retires because she will no longer be saving for retirement or paying Social Security tax and assorted other work-related expenses. She factors in higher health care costs, but this is balanced out by her plan to be debt-free by retirement age. She has dreams, of course, but for this exercise, we are just looking for the minimum level of income needed. Remember, this is in today's dollars.

> It is far better to foresee even without certainty than not to foresee at all.
> —Henri Poincaré

Counting Your Chicks Before They Hatch

The next step is to determine how many golden eggs will have to be in your baskets to maintain your current standard of living. Begin by adding up all your anticipated retirement income from sources other than investments. If you're like most of us, this will probably be a fairly short list. If you have a traditional pension plan, write down your expected annual benefit amount. You should be able to get this from your benefits manager or plan administrator at work. If you will be eligible for Social Security benefits, list that annual amount. Use the statement you receive from Social Security each year. If you don't have it, you can request a statement online at www.socialsecurity.gov or by calling 1-800-772-1213. The website also has calculators to help you decide when to start your bene-

Designing Your Henhouse

fits as well as information on how to apply. Use Worksheet 3: Estimate of Retirement Income for this task. Here's Ima's:

Worksheet 3: Estimate of Retirement Income

Estimate of Retirement Income	
Pension	$ 8,828
Social Security	$ 17,172
	$
	$
	$
Total annual income expected	$ 26,000

Fig. 3: Ima Investor's Worksheet

Add up your list and enter the total in Column B of Worksheet 4: Finding Your Number. Now simply subtract your estimated expenses from your estimated annual income and enter that amount in Column C. This is the amount you will need to withdraw from your investment accounts each year to meet your minimum income level. Ima estimates her retirement income to be $26,000. Here is her Worksheet 4 so far:

Worksheet 4: Finding Your Number

COLUMN A	COLUMN B	COLUMN C
Income Needed	Retirement Income from Worsheet 3	Annual Portfolio Withdrawal
$42,500	$26,000	$16,500

Finding Your Number

Now you know how much you will need to withdraw from your portfolio to supplement your other sources of income, but not your target net worth—your "number." In other words, how many hens will you have to keep in your henhouse to ensure an adequate supply of eggs? In my research, I found many financial experts recommend withdrawing no more than four percent of retirement savings each year to avoid running out of money. Some go as high as six percent, but the percentage to use is related to your age at the time you begin withdrawals and the state of the economy. People with longer time horizons, say thirty years or so, are wise not to exceed four percent, although those who are older and have shorter time horizons can go as high as six percent in relative safety depending on market conditions. Because it seems to be one of the rare factors upon which there is agreement, I suggest you use four percent for your calculations.

Since you are reading this book, I'm going to assume crunching more numbers is not your idea of a good time, so I'm going to give you the easiest way to arrive at your number:

Divide the annual amount you want to withdraw by four percent.

That's it—simple enough? Ima has determined she will need to withdraw $16,500 annually to meet her basic needs. To calculate how much should be in her portfolio to allow her to stay within the four percent annual withdrawal guideline, she divides $16,500 by .04 and finds she will need a portfolio value of $412,500. This amount goes in Column D of her Worksheet 4.

Taking Inventory

Let's go one step further and determine how much you need to add to your portfolio to reach your goal. To find this, simply subtract the total amount you have already saved from your number in Column D. If you made your list of assets from the first chapter, use that, but unless you are planning on renting a home or living in a Winnebago the rest of your life, do not include the equity of your house. The money you made from that sale would have to be reinvested in another home. If you haven't made your list, go ahead and do it now. When you have finished, enter the amount in Column E, then subtract it from Column D, and record your answer in Column F.

Designing Your Henhouse

Ima has managed to accumulate $150,000 in her portfolio, which consists of her 401(k), a couple of mutual funds, and some assorted bonds. She fills in three more columns on her Worksheet 4:

Worksheet 4: Finding Your Number

COLUMN D	COLUMN E	COLUMN F
Portfolio Required	Current Portfolio	Increase Needed
$412,500	$150,000	$262,500

See? This isn't so hard. But the amounts you have just calculated are what you would need if you retired *now*. We know prices increase due to that nasty little critter called inflation, and a dollar today will be worth much less in the future (another reason why procrastinating about investing is a bad idea). You need to get an idea of how much you will need *later*. To make this calculation, you will need two additional pieces of data:

1. The number of years remaining until you plan to retire.
2. An estimated annual rate of inflation. Most financial planners use three percent, and that is what I used in the example that follows. You can use a different rate if you would like.

Ima's target retirement age is sixty-five. She is now forty years old, so she wants to know what her annual withdrawal amount will be in twenty-five years adjusted for inflation. Into an online inflation calculator, she enters the amount from Column C, an inflation rate and the number of years until retirement and *voila*—she has her answer. Ima finds that twenty-five years into the future, her annual withdrawal amount will be $34,547.34. Some useful websites for this are www.calculatorweb.com and www.hellodollar.com.

Now, just as she did before, she divides her annual withdrawal amount by .04 (a four percent withdrawal rate) to arrive at the desired value of her portfolio adjusted for inflation. She now knows how many future dollars she wants to have in her portfolio at the time she retires. Here are the final two columns on her Worksheet 4:

INVESTING STARTING FROM SCRATCH

Worksheet 4: Finding Your Number

COLUMN G	COLUMN H
Annual Withdrawal in Future Dollars	Total Portfolio in Future Dollars
$34,547	$863,683

Ima's completed Worksheet 4 is shown in Table 1.

Dreaming About What You Want

So far, we have talked about meeting your needs, but what about your dreams? Before you invest a single dime, now is the time for you to do a little soul searching. Put this book down for awhile. Sit quietly and let your mind relax. Imagine your ideal lifestyle—what would it be like? Here are some questions to get you started:

> One of the biggest impediments to getting what you want in life is not knowing what that is.
> —JERROLD MUNDIS

- Where would you like to live? Would it require a move?
- How would you spend your time?
- What activities would you most enjoy doing?
- How expensive are your desired pastimes?
- Would you work full-time or part-time?
- Is it important to you to leave money to heirs? To favorite charities or organizations?
- Is your vision realistic? If not, how can you modify it to make it so?

Perhaps your retirement plans include travel, adventure, indulging in art or theatre, or other expensive pastimes. If so, make your best guess of realistic costs for these activities and add the figures to your basic budget. If your dream life involves moving to another area, you will need to get some actual costs of living there. Check such things as housing prices and the cost of food, fuel, and utilities. The internet has made this research much simpler than it used to be. This is an important first step, so please don't skip it. If you wanted to plan a trip, the first thing you would do is decide where you want to go. Then you would consult a map to determine how far it is to your destination. With this information, you could calculate how long it would take to get there and how much the trip would cost. Setting a life course is no different, but many of us just wander aimlessly toward our older years with no particular destination in mind. This brings to mind a bit of folk wisdom I once heard which said, "You'd better watch where you're going, or you'll end up where you're headed." Take the time to decide where you want to go.

> You'd better watch where you are going or you will end up where you are headed.
> —Author Unknown

Ima has big dreams of buying a house on the beach. She envisions spending blissful days sailing a sleek little sloop and quiet evenings watching the sunset from her balcony while sipping frosty Margaritas. Being somewhat methodical—and good at following instructions—she has worked through all her formulas again for her dream budget and estimates she can live out her dreams on an annual income of $62,000. You can see her completed worksheet in Table 2.

A Reality Check

Ima contributes ten percent of her current gross salary every month to her retirement accounts, or in round figures, about $5,000 annually. Will she have enough to make her dream come true? To answer this question, she needs to know the return she would have to make on her investments. Ima consults her financial planner to find out how well her hens would have to produce to achieve her goals. She learns she will need a return of about six percent from all her investments in order to reach her desired minimum goal. Is this achievable? The odds are in her favor. How about the ten percent it will take to reach her dream goal? Doubtful, unless she has quite a bit of luck on her side.

If your required return is much higher than six to eight percent, it is probably time to make some adjustments in your planning. Better to face the painful truth now rather than later when you may not be in a position to make course corrections. One caveat: Many times, you will hear from financial professionals that you will need less money when you retire. Maybe, maybe not. They base this opinion on several things: your mortgage—usually your single largest expense—has probably been paid off, you will save money on clothes, commuting, lunches out and other business-related expenses, and you will no longer contribute to retirement plans or pay payroll taxes. All of this is true; however, many people spend *more* in retirement because they have the time to travel and engage in hobbies—sometimes expensive ones—and, in your later years, health care costs may take a significant bite out of your budget. Whether you spend more or less in retirement depends entirely on your lifestyle.

Playing the Odds at Monte Carlo

Every financial ad you see or hear will include a disclaimer that states, "past performance is not indicative of future results," or words to that effect. That is because life is not predictable and orderly. Life does not move in a straight line, and neither do the markets. If they did, no one would ever lose money in them and this would not all seem so complicated. Unfortunately, the spreadsheet (which you have just so laboriously constructed) *does* move in a straight line. It tells you what would happen if things happened exactly the way you predicted. It is still a good place to start, but financial professionals use a method called *Monte Carlo Modeling* to simulate multiple scenarios and arrive at a range of possible outcomes.

Developed by scientists as a tool to measure probabilities, this sophisticated program looks at a large number of variables such as your age, lifestyle and life expectancy, as well as assumptions about investment returns such as your tax rate, varying rates of inflation and the effect of various asset allocations. You can buy the software to do this yourself, but there is really no need. There are several financial websites which allow you to plug in your numbers and they do all the work. Here are just a few places to find retirement guidance and advice:

Designing Your Henhouse

- Vanguard (www.vanguard.com)
- T. Rowe Price (www.troweprice.com)
- Fidelity (www.fidelity.com). They require you to register to use the site, but it's free.

You have already learned that investing is not an exact science, so you will find different programs that yield different results and recommendations. In addition, there are factors we haven't discussed here that will affect your planning, such as income taxes on withdrawals from retirement funds and lump-sum distributions. A qualified financial professional who knows the right questions to ask can be invaluable in helping you create a plan.

How Long Do You Have To Gather Your Eggs?

The investing needs of someone age thirty and just getting started and the needs of someone contemplating retirement are very different indeed. The younger investor can take on more risk because she has time to recover from a poorly-performing investment. Someone older and living on a fixed income needs the security of a surer thing, so she will probably choose more conservative investment vehicles. Speaking of time, none of us knows exactly how much of that precious commodity we have. Wouldn't it be great if you knew exactly how many years your savings had to last? Then you would know whether to spend your money conservatively or blow it all on one last trip to Fiji. On second thought, maybe that wouldn't be so great. There are some life expectancy calculators out there if you want to take a look, but for figuring your future financial needs, why not plan for a nice, long life? Most financial advisors use a minimum life expectancy of ninety-five years.

> A goal without a plan is just a wish.
>
> —Antoine De Saint-Exupery

What Kind of Hen Keeper Are You? Your Investing Style

We all want the same thing—enough golden eggs to last the rest of our lives, but we will not all go about accumulating them the same way. My mother used to say, "It is a wise person who knows and accepts herself," and as usual, she was right. Your investment strategy must fit your personality. Are you a get-to-the-bottom-line person? Or the methodical researcher type? Do you get an adrenaline rush by taking risks? Or do you like to keep things on a nice, even keel? It's important to be honest with yourself because you are the one who won't sleep at night if you don't listen to your inner voice.

Regardless of personality type, we all strive to preserve our capital—no one wants to lose money—and we all want to see our capital grow, but there is no one *right* way to achieve your objectives. There is no guaranteed way, either—no matter what the infomercials or salespeople at the free lunch seminars say.

> There is always free cheese in a mousetrap.
> —Mark Skousen

The portfolio of a person with a conservative investment strategy will be weighted with more fixed-income securities such as bonds and money market instruments, while the portfolio of a person with a more aggressive investment strategy will contain more stocks. In either type, there must still be plenty of diversity to help minimize risk. Be honest with yourself here—are you a tortoise or a hare? And remember who won the race.

Having Enough Baskets: Modern Portfolio Theory

"Don't put all your eggs in one basket." Only someone growing up on Mars hasn't received this piece of advice at one time or another in her life, but an economist named Harry Markowitz developed a whole theory around the idea in 1952 and won a Nobel Prize for it in 1990. He used many calculations involving standard deviations that make for very interesting reading—if you are an economist. For the rest of us, the main idea of *Modern Portfolio Theory* is this: If you select a combination of well-researched investments of different types for your portfolio, you reduce your risk of loss. Here's an example: Suppose you own two investments. One pays off if the rooster crows in the morning and one pays off if he doesn't. Either way, your portfolio won't lose. This is diversifying in a nutshell.

Designing Your Henhouse

> Some people think they are diversified by holding several mutual funds. I did—until I checked what those mutual funds were holding and discovered the same stocks in all of them!

Nailing It All Down

If you have not been a diligent saver, don't let these big numbers discourage you. Some surveys report only one out of every four workers over the age of fifty-five has an investment portfolio worth more than $100,000. The purpose of this exercise is to establish a direction so you can set realistic goals. Ima, for example, has discovered she will probably not be able to fund her dream lifestyle and some changes are in order. Some of the options open to her are:

- Consult a qualified financial planner to make sure her portfolio is allocated for optimal performance.
- Increase her income. She can try to earn more money by asking for a raise, taking a second job, changing jobs or maybe even her career.
- Save more. She can increase the amount of her contributions to her retirement accounts and make sure she is taking advantage of any available employer matches.
- Adjust her dreams. She can decide she doesn't have to live right on the beach, and she can buy a used boat or even charter one when she wants to sail.
- She can delay her retirement for a few more years.
- She can continue working either full or part-time after age sixty-five to make up the deficits.

Surveys show the two most common worries people have about retirement are getting sick and outliving their money. Chances are these concerns have crossed your mind a time or two, so let's tackle these demons head on:

- Withdrawing too much from your savings too soon is the fastest road to zero. Knowing how much you can safely withdraw when the time comes will protect you from financial disaster.

- Inflation eats up your savings quickly because the value of your portfolio is decreasing while prices are increasing—a double whammy. For example, if you invested in a CD that earned four percent, and then had to pay bank fees and taxes on your earnings, you could end up with less than you started with. Maintaining a reasonable asset allocation will help you stay ahead of inflation.
- Take care of yourself and plan for a long tenure here. You don't want to outlive your money, but you don't want to be the richest resident in the retirement home, either, dreaming of what could have been. Creating your financial plan is about finding balance between security and a meaningful existence.

Now that you have constructed your henhouse, are you ready to shop for hens? Good. Let's go to market.

THE BOTTOM LINE

- You are the most important factor in any financial plan: your values, hopes and dreams.
- The first step in designing your plan is to determine your current cost of living, then your budget for your retirement dream life (what it would cost if you could do it today).
- The second step is to estimate your retirement income from all sources other than your investment portfolio.
- The third step is to determine how much of your income needs to come from your investments.
- The fourth step is to calculate your number, or the total amount needed in your portfolio at retirement to maintain a reasonable withdrawal rate.
- The fifth step is to find how much more money you will need to add to your savings prior to retirement.
- The sixth step is to factor in inflation. How much will your number be at the time you want to retire?
- The last step is to determine if your portfolio will be adequate to fund your retirement. If not, some revisions are in order.
- Monte Carlo Modeling is a sophisticated planning tool that

> Wishing consumes as much energy as planning.
>
> —AUTHOR UNKNOWN

takes many variables into account to yield a range of possible outcomes.
- Your investing style and time frame will have an impact on your planning.
- Modern Portfolio Theory is the basis of diversification.

> Former Governor of Texas Ann Richards was a strong advocate of financial education for women. When asked about her personal financial goals, she quipped, "My financial goal is not to end up in a trailer in my daughter's driveway."

INVESTING STARTING FROM SCRATCH

TABLE 1
Ima Investor's Minimum Needs Projections
Age: 40
Years to retirement: 25

Column A	Column B	Column C	Column D	Column E	Column F	Column G	Column H
Income Needed	Retirement Income from Worksheet 1	Annual Portfolio Withdrawal	Portfolio Required	Current Portfolio	Increase Needed	Annual W/D in Future Dollars	Total Portfolio in Future Dollars
$42,500.00	$26,000.00	$16,500.00	$412,500.00	$150,000.00	$262,500.00	$34,547.34	$863,683.50

Her net worth now

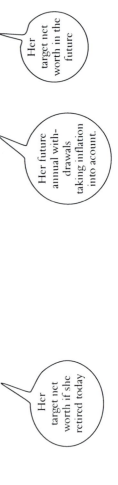

Her target net worth if she retired today

Her future annual withdrawals taking inflation into acount.

Her target net worth in the future

28

Designing Your Henhouse

TABLE 2
Ima Investor's Dream Life Projections
Age: 40
Years to retirement: 25

Column A	Column B	Column C	Column D	Column E	Column F	Column G	Column H
Income Needed	Retirement Income from Worksheet 1	Annual Portfolio Withdrawal	Portfolio Required	Current Portfolio	Increase Needed	Annual W/D in Future Dollars	Total Portfolio in Future Dollars
$62,000.00	$26,000.00	$36,000.00	$900,000.00	$150,000.00	$750,000.00	$75,376.01	$1,884,400.25

"Stocks were down today, but bounced back after someone drove down Wall Street throwing Prozac from the back of a truck."

CHAPTER THREE

Buying Hens at the Stock Market

ALTHOUGH WE REFER to the stock market as if it were a single place on Wall Street, in reality there are multiple marketplaces, called *stock exchanges*. In the United States, The New York Stock Exchange (NYSE) and the American Stock Exchange (AMEX) are auction-based marketplaces. They are housed in brick and mortar buildings with trading floors where traders buy and sell stock in verbal auctions. The National Association of Securities Dealers Automated Quotations, better known as the NASDAQ, is an electronic exchange which means buyers and sellers are connected by computer—the floor of the NASDAQ is virtual. Wall Street is the original home of the New York Stock Exchange, but today when we speak of this famous street, we are referring to the financial and investment community collectively rather than a specific address. Stocks found on the U.S. stock exchanges represent just a fraction of the total. There are many other stock exchanges located around the world.

The Securities and Exchange Commission (SEC) is a federal regulatory agency created in 1934. The SEC's main function is to monitor the securities industry to protect the public from the kinds of speculation and abuses that led to the stock market crash in 1929. It is composed of five commissioners, appointed by the U.S. President. These commissioners create and amend rules, interpret securities laws and

> Wall Street got its name from a twelve foot high wooden stockade erected across the rivers in Manhattan by Dutch settlers in 1653 to protect them from attack by the British and the Indians.

oversee all firms, brokers, and investment advisors. In essence, they are the supreme court in the land of investing.*

What Is Stock?

When a private company decides to issue stock, it "goes public" by placing ownership of the company in the hands of investors, rather than in those of a few private owners. Most of the time this is done to raise capital to allow the company to grow. Company officials work with investment bankers who register the required information with the SEC and also act as underwriters. The underwriters work with the company to determine the offering price of the stock and then assume responsibility for initial sales. The first sale of shares to the public is referred to as the *Initial Public Offering* or IPO. This is generally preceded by press releases and a lot of media attention. After the IPO is completed, shares begin to trade—they are sold and bought and bought and sold—ad infinitum in the secondary market. It is easy to see why they call it a stock *exchange*.

> **Although it's easy to forget sometimes, a share of stock is not a lottery ticket. It's part ownership of a business.**
> —PETER LYNCH

The two types of stock are *preferred* and *common*. A common stockholder (aka shareholder) has a claim to part of the company's assets and earnings. The total number of shares issued determines the amount of an individual's ownership. Here is an example: A company issues 100,000 shares of stock and you buy 1,000 shares. That means you own one percent of the company—just like that, you're in business! You are entitled to attend shareholder meetings, vote to elect members of the board of directors and receive *dividends* if they are declared. Dividends represent the portion of the company's net profit that is divided among its owners. On the flip side, you also assume part of the risk of doing business. If the company loses money or goes bankrupt, your investment goes down the drain, too.

---

* The SEC has suffered serious blows to its reputation in the past year because of its failure to recognize wide-spread abuses in the stock market. The future of this agency is undetermined, but certainly there will be changes.

Preferred stock is in a separate class issued with different rules that vary from company to company. In essence, preferred stockholders are at the front of the line. They usually receive dividends guaranteed at a fixed rate before dividends are paid to common shareholders. They also have a higher claim on assets than common shareholders in the event a company fails—if there are any assets left after the banks, bond holders and other creditors take their shares. In exchange for this preferential treatment they usually forfeit their right to vote and have reduced potential for gains.

Learning Your Way Around the Market

There are thousands of stocks available for purchase just in the U.S. markets alone. The task of choosing what to buy from the entire marketplace would be formidable without some way to divide them into manageable categories. The most common are size, industry and sector.

Size
Companies are classified by their size or total value of all outstanding (owned or on the market for sale) shares. This is commonly referred to as *market capitalization* or market cap. Parameters change over time, but as a general rule, here are the definitions:

- Large-cap companies have market caps over $10 billion
- Mid-cap companies have market caps of $2 billion to $10 billion
- Small-cap companies have market caps of $300 million to $2 billion

Large-cap companies are huge companies such as Microsoft, Coca-Cola, and Wal-Mart. Many of these stocks are referred to as *Blue Chips* because of their solid track records. These mature companies maintain a steady level of sales but are likely to grow more slowly. Why? Because the main ways a company grows are by moving into new markets or by making new products. Coke, for example, is already in almost every country in the world and is not likely to introduce many new products. Remember their *New Coke* attempt? That was more than twenty years ago. Customers were quick to let them know they didn't want the formula changed, so Coca-Cola wisely gave people what they wanted—the old Coca-Cola they loved. Since these large caps are making handsome profits and do not need all of it to reinvest in their growth, they send the excess to their shareholders in the form of lovely dividend checks. Coca-Cola, for example, has paid quarterly dividends every year since 1920.

Mid-cap companies have been around awhile, but still have room to grow. Again, they can expand by introducing new products, entering new markets, or merging with other companies. *Small-cap* companies are often the newbies. If they succeed—and many do not—they are going to be the fastest growers. In order to attract investors, these companies must show higher returns to compensate for the increased risk.

Industry and sector

Companies of all three sizes can be found in different types of industries. A sector is a group of companies in the same industry. The ten industries, created using The Global Industrial Classification Standard or GICS include:

- Materials
- Industrials
- Energy
- Utilities
- Telecommunications
- Consumer discretionary
- Consumer staples
- Health care
- Financial
- Information technology

Stock classifications are very useful when you are considering companies to buy because business types have vastly different profit margins. For instance, it would not be useful to compare a grocery chain stock with a normal profit margin of five percent or less to that of a retail specialty stock that earns profits in the double digits. Classifications ensure you are comparing apples to apples.

A diversified stock portfolio is made up of an assortment of stocks of different-sized companies selected from several industries. This is a very good thing, as your eggs are in different baskets. Of course, a portfolio is further diversified when it also contains bonds, cash and real estate—but we will get to that a bit later.

How Investors Make Money in the Stock Market

There are two main ways investors earn returns in the stock market. The first is through dividends, or the portion of the company's net profit that is divided among owners. Dividends are usually—but not always—paid by mature, stable companies who have reached the peak of their growth. Some experts refer to these stocks as "stalwarts."

> One of the funny things about the stock market is that every time one person buys, another sells, and both think they are astute.
> —WILLIAM FEATHER

The second way is through price appreciation. Investors buy stock with the anticipation that at some point in the future it will be worth more and then they will be able to sell their shares at a profit. Stocks form the foundation of nearly any investment portfolio for a number of reasons:

- They are liquid, which means you can buy and sell them easily.
- There is no price ambiguity. You know what they are worth at any moment of the day—in fact, these days you can hardly escape the incessant ticker tape displays scrolling across the bottom of television screens and popping up on your computer screen.
- Stocks have the best record among investment vehicles of outpacing inflation and creating solid returns over the long term.

Stocks are no longer the ticket to wealth for the privileged few. With the transition to self-directed retirement planning and the advent of online trading tools, it has become simpler to own them. Since stocks are not without risk, it is essential to have a basic understanding of how they work so you won't fall prey to the latest hot tip or pseudo-advisor. One of the keys to success in the stock market is to understand what you are buying and *why*. With that in mind, how do you select these hens? There are two broad methods investors use to study stocks being considered for purchase: fundamental and technical analysis. We will look at each of them individually in the next section.

Shopping Strategies

Fundamental Analysis

Fundamental analysis focuses on the intrinsic value of a company. If someone approached you and asked you to invest in a business, you might be interested, but it is unlikely you would hand over a check without first gathering some data. You would want to understand exactly what kind of business it is, what product or service is being offered and how much profit is expected. You would also want to have confidence in the company's leadership and know how much of the managers' own capital has been contributed to the venture. This is fundamental analysis in a nutshell.

> Investing without research is like playing stud poker and never looking at the cards.
> —Peter Lynch

A fundamental analyst will look at a company's past in order to gauge its future performance. She will examine financial statements and quarterly reports and use historical data to analyze sales and earnings performance. She will investigate the management team and assess their ability to lead the company in a positive direction. She will be very interested in knowing how much of the company's stock is personally owned by its officers and directors. When senior managers hold stock in their own portfolios, particularly if they have purchased it on the open market and not simply received it through the exercise of stock options, it not only demonstrates confidence in the company, it is an additional incentive for the management team to operate the company profitably. A fundamental analyst also looks at any other factors that might affect a stock, such as overall economic and political conditions. Finally, she looks at the price of the stock.

No matter how good a company is, the price of the stock in relation to its value is a key determining factor in whether a fundamental analyst buys it or not. The company is valued using several tools. The *price to earnings* (P/E) *ratio*, also referred to as *price multiple* or *earnings multiple*, indicates how much confidence investors have in the stock's growth prospects. This is calculated by dividing the market value (price) of a stock by its annual earnings per share. The *PEG ratio* adds in growth factors. It is calculated by dividing the P/E ratio by the annual growth of earnings per share. That's enough of that—I don't want to overburden you with the mechanics. Rome wasn't built in a day and neither is a portfolio. If you want to learn more about this type of stock analysis, there are many resources to help you become proficient. Check out Better Investing, formerly known as the National Association of Investors Corporation (NAIC), at www.betterinvesting.org and the American Association of Individual Investors at www.aaii.com. These nonprofit organizations are dedicated to providing financial education and support for individual investors. Both have many excellent and affordable learning tools to help you master fundamental analysis skills. They hold regular meetings where you can find like-minded people, so check to see if there is a meeting location near you.

Technical Analysis

Technical analysis is based on the premise that price patterns and trends exist in the market. Believing that history repeats itself, technicians use past information to forecast future price trends. They do not study the fundamentals of individual companies that make up the market, but rather focus their attention on the market itself. They use charts and other tools to analyze price movements and then this data is used to forecast future directions. Direction of movement is the all-important factor; the reasons *why* a stock is rising or falling are irrelevant to the technical analyst.

> Don't let the name fool you—technical analysis is not a modern technique. The Japanese were using candlestick charting to trade rice in the seventeenth century.

The motto of a technician or "chartist" is "the trend is your friend." A trend line is simply a line on a chart that indicates movement. Trends appear as zigzag patterns as the stock price fluctuates, but the pattern will generally move in a direction: up, down or horizontally. These are called, appropriately enough, "uptrends," "downtrends," or "sideways trends." The level a stock does not fall below on the chart is referred to as "support," and the level a stock does not rise above is referred to as "resistance." A "channel" is created between these two levels by the addition of two parallel trend lines.

There are different types of charts used by technical analysts, but the main ones are line, bar, candlestick, and point and figure charts. They have colorful names for different patterns formed by stock price movements, such as "head and shoulders," "cup and handle," "flags and pennants," and "rounding bottom." Technicians also use *moving averages* to help make sense of price fluctuation patterns, which they refer to as "noise." A moving average is the average of a security's price over a specified period of time. Successful traders who buy low and sell high are said to have "strong hands" or to be the "smart money."

Is There a "Correct" Way?

The short answer to this question is no. Investing is not an exact science and the method you decide to use to analyze stocks depends on your goals and what makes the most sense to you. Frequently, investors who buy stocks and hold them for a long time use fundamental analysis while traders who buy and sell quickly are more likely to use technical analysis. Many see these two methods as complete opposites, but some investors use both as a way to look at stocks from all angles. We have barely scratched the surface of these methods. There is enough information about each to fill volumes and indeed, there are many books on the shelves at your local bookstore. My hope is that you now know what you are looking for if you want to learn more.

Just as there are different ways to analyze stocks, there are also different strategies employed by stock-pickers. *Growth investors* focus on earnings—these are buy and hold people. They look for fairly-priced, growing companies with the best earning potential. A growth investor's portfolio may be concentrated more in small-cap stocks, in the hope that one or more of them will become the next Microsoft. Small-cap stocks, as you now know, have the potential for great returns, but they also involve more risk because of the high failure rate of new companies. Careful homework is essential and finding enough information for a new company without much history can be a challenge.

Value investors are bargain hunters. Like the shoppers who try to find designer jeans on the sale rack, they look for stocks that are underpriced in relation to their performance and long-term fundamentals. They believe the market overreacts to good and bad news, causing stock prices to get out of sync with reality. Warren Buffet is probably the most famous value investor. He also uses fundamental analysis methods and eschews trading. He has been quoted as saying his favorite time to sell a stock is never.

Income investors seek current income in the form of dividends, interest, or other payments. These investors are likely to be retirees. Their portfolios will probably contain more Blue Chip stocks along with bonds (in the next chapter), and REITs, which we will discuss shortly.

> Most of what goes on in the market is very random . . . there isn't always an explanation for what's happening. But people want to hear a story.
> —JEREMY SIEGEL

Why Do Stock Prices Change?

More often than not, stock prices are affected by the dynamics of supply and demand. There is a limited supply of shares, so the more people that want to buy them, the higher the price goes—sort of like real estate in Hawaii. This is the reason technology stock prices were off the chart during the 1990s. Everybody wanted in on the action, so the prices were way out of proportion to the value of the stock.

Earnings (or profits) are the single most important factor that affect the value of a company. All publicly-traded companies must make their financial reports public on a quarterly basis. In advance of the posting date, stock analysts make estimates of what they think the earnings will be. If the company reports are better than the analysts' projections, the stock price may go up; if they are worse than the projections, the stock price may go down—even if the difference is only a penny or two.

Finally, there is just plain emotion involved. The non-stop news about stocks and other world events has an impact on investor sentiments. When the news is good, prices may go up, and when the news is negative, prices may go down. Companies and whole industries fall out of favor, sometimes for no apparent reason.

The bottom line is that a stock's price indicates what the buying public thinks it is worth. It is based on the current value of a company and on the growth investors expect to see. You must learn to decide for yourself whether to buy or sell an equity. It is a good idea to make notes to yourself as to why you decided to buy a stock so you will not be caught up in the latest hype or swayed by media frenzy.

What Are Stock Splits?

Sometimes the price of a stock goes so high it discourages investors from buying. To make share prices more attractive, the company divides existing shares and declares a *stock split*. A two-for-one split means the investor who owned one share now owns two. A four-for-one split means the investor who owned one share now owns four. The number of shares increases, but their total value remains unchanged. The company has simply divided the same pie into smaller pieces.

A company can also declare a *reverse stock split*, which means a decrease in the number of existing shares. A one-for-two reverse split means an investor who owned two shares now owns one, which effectively doubles the price for the remaining share. This usually indicates bad news because companies often do this to make their stock look more valuable than it is or to retain their listing on an exchange that requires a certain minimum price per share.

What Kinds of Returns Can I Expect?

I wish I could give you a number, but again the answer is—it depends. It depends on whether you are investing in a bull market or a bear market. It depends on if you stay invested in the market or trade in and out. It depends on your investment time frame. Historically, the average annual return from the U.S. stock market has been ten to twelve percent but that does not mean you can reasonably expect to put your money in the market and reap this nice return. A study from the University of Michigan concluded that an investor who stayed invested in the market the entire time from 1963 to 1993 would have earned an average annual return of almost twelve percent. But investors who were in the market all but the best ninety days out of that thirty-year period earned only a little over three percent annually.*

We experienced a long bear market in the United States from 1966 to 1982 where the average investor with an average portfolio who stayed fully invested in the market lost twenty-two percent. Bummer. But, from 1982 until 1999, the average total return was a whopping eighteen percent.

> What can't go on forever—won't.
> —WALL STREET PROVERB

During that period people ignored historical lessons and started to believe stocks meant instant wealth. Indeed, many did become "dot-com millionaires." Unfortunately, when the tech bubble burst, many of these nouveau riche were turned back into pumpkins.

As I write this, we're in the midst of financial free-fall as a result of the credit crisis and unregulated capitalism. Many investors are again experiencing negative returns, and the end is not yet in sight—despite the federal government's efforts to shore up the markets. When sales people show you charts, they always point out that, over time, the market has had its ups and downs, but it has continued to rise. Stocks can be good, long-term investments. Deciding how much of your savings to invest in the market depends on how much time you have to recover from these downturns.

How to Make a Purchase

Historically, the most common way to buy stocks has been through a stockbroker. Stockbrokers in the United States must be licensed through FINRA (Financial Industry Regulatory Authority).** They work for brokerage firms and act as the intermediaries between the stock exchange and you. There are different types of firms as well as different kinds of accounts, and more new choices seem to appear weekly. Whether you choose a full-service broker who will provide investment advice or a discount brokerage where everything is handled online, the steps to buy stock are the same. Here is how it works:

---

* From *Stock Market Extremes and Portfolio Performance* by Professor H. Nejat Seyhun, University of Michigan, commissioned by Towneley Capital Management.
** Formerly the NASD (National Association of Securities Dealers) was responsible for this, but NASD and the New York Stock Exchange regulators merged to form FINRA in 2007.

INVESTING STARTING FROM SCRATCH

1. First, you open an account at a brokerage firm and deposit funds. Firms have different terms and conditions and some require a minimum balance, so read the fine print and check those fees.
2. You decide to purchase stock in ABC Corporation (after doing your homework, of course). If yours is a full-service firm, you call your broker, tell her how many shares you want, and she executes your *market order*. A market order means you will pay the market price at the time the transaction is completed. Prices can change very rapidly, so it may not be the same price as the one in effect at the time you placed your order. If you want to discuss the stock with your broker first, go ahead—that is what you are paying for. If yours is a discount brokerage, you generally will place your order online and unassisted.
3. The brokerage sends a confirmation of your purchase, either electronically or by mail.

That's all there is to it. Well, actually there is more to it if you want to place conditions on your purchase, such as stop orders or limit orders, but that is a subject for a more advanced book.

You will not receive paper stock certificates from your broker because the stock is held in the name of the brokerage, or in *street name*. You will be listed as the beneficial owner and you will receive statements of all transactions. This arrangement is common and makes transferring shares much easier. Imagine the logistics of constantly mailing stock certificates back and forth as shares are bought and sold—this practice has all but been eliminated.

Whether you choose a full-service broker or a discount broker is largely a matter of your personal style. Traders usually prefer a discount brokerage with low trading fees. A buy-and-hold investor who does not execute many trades will be more concerned with account maintenance fees. Regardless of the type of brokerage you want, there are some useful websites that will help you to check them out. The most comprehensive is FINRA's BrokerCheck at www.finra.org. The J.D. Power Awards site at www.jdpower.com (click on the "Finance" tab) offers a ratings chart of investment firms based on their research. If you want to read opinions from other investors, you can find customer reviews posted on www.epinions.com about brokerages, financial websites, and a number of other personal finance concerns.

Make sure the brokerage you choose is a member of the *Securities Investor Protection Corporation*. The SIPC is a non-profit corporation funded by its member broker-dealers that is designed to protect investors if a brokerage becomes insolvent. When a member brokerage goes bankrupt or becomes financially unstable—as we've seen recently with the collapse of some of our largest institutions—the SIPC works with trustees to liquidate the firm and distribute the assets to claimants. Investors may recover up to a maximum of $500,000 in securities and a maximum of $100,000 in cash. The SIPC does not combat fraud and it does not cover all investments, but it does cover stock. It also does not protect against market risk—there are no guarantees in the stock market.

> **It is only the farmer who faithfully plants seeds in the Spring, who reaps a harvest in the Autumn.**
> —B.C. FORBES

DIPS and DRIPS

Another way to buy stocks is from the source. Some companies will sell directly to investors, usually without any additional commissions or fees attached. You may see this referred to as *DIP* (Direct Investment Plan), *DSPP* (Direct Stock Purchase Plan) or as *DESP* (Direct Enrollment Stock Purchase Plan). If you have limited funds to invest, this can be an excellent way to get started because you can open some accounts with as little as $100. Often these accounts include a *DRIP* option (Dividend Reinvestment Plan), which enables you to reinvest any earnings and buy more stock instead of receiving a distribution from the company when dividends are paid. You can also send a little extra to the company to be added to your dividend payment; these are referred to as *OCP* or Optional Cash Payments. If this method interests you, a good place to begin your research into companies that have DRIP plans is www.stockselector.com.

Not all companies with DRIP plans have direct purchase plans. Some require you to make the initial stock purchase through a broker. In these cases, the investor must be the *shareholder of record*, which means the stock certificate is held in your name and not the street name of the brokerage. This way, the company is notified that you are a shareholder and then you can enroll in their DRIP. After that, all contact is directly with the company. It generally costs more to open a broker-assisted DRIP than it does to buy a DIP.

DIPS are a low cost way to invest. There are no broker fees, except for possibly the original purchase, no annual fees, and no advertising fees. Transaction fees, if any, are very low and many charge no fees at all. The disadvantages of DIPs and DRIPs are you must keep your own records and most of the time, if you want to sell shares, you must make a written request. The companies that court direct investors do so because they are looking for long-term, stable shareholders. They are also looking for loyal customers, so it is not uncommon for companies to include discount coupons with their annual reports. Some companies offer discounts on their reinvestment purchases. DIPs and DRIPS can be a great way to teach kids about investing. You can involve them in the stock research and let them pick the companies they like. With enough time, small amounts turn into big amounts thanks to the miracle of compounding. Remember our lowly penny example in Chapter One.

While we are on the subject of pennies, a word is in order on *penny stocks*. These stocks don't actually sell for one cent, but for many, that is about what they are worth. These are highly speculative (read: risky) issues of companies that are sold outside of the stock exchanges. That means they have few, if any, regulatory standards. They are not for beginning investors—and that is my two cents' worth on the subject.

> Wisely and slow. They stumble that run fast.
> —SHAKESPEARE

Other Animals in the Barnyard

When things in the economy are going great and stocks are on the upswing, we have a bull market. During the tech stock boom, the bull market was roaring full speed and it was difficult—but not impossible—to lose money. People lost sight of historical lessons learned and threw caution to the wind. It is thrilling to run with the bulls as long as you keep a wary eye out for the bears. When the economy takes a downturn and stock prices are falling, the bears have

Buying Hens at the Stock Market

moved in. Finding profitable stocks in a bear market is much more difficult—but not impossible.

Chickens are so afraid of losing money that they never invest at all. The irony is unless they at least put their savings in the money market, they lose anyway through inflation. And pigs? They are the ones who buy on hot tips and look for the quick road to riches.

> Bulls make money, bears make money, but pigs just get slaughtered.
> —WALL STREET PROVERB

"People with big heads need to invest in large cap stocks. People with small heads should invest in small cap stocks. Investing is easy if you know what you're doing!"

INVESTING STARTING FROM SCRATCH

THE BOTTOM LINE

- The stock market is not a physical place, but rather the name used for the collective stock exchanges.
- A company issues its first shares through an IPO. After that, shares are traded in the secondary market or stock exchange.
- Companies are classified by their size or total value of all outstanding (owned or on the market for sale) shares. This is commonly referred to as market capitalization or "market cap."
- The key to success in the stock market is to understand what you are buying and most importantly, why you are buying it.
- Fundamental analysis focuses on the intrinsic value of a company.
- Technical analysis is based on price patterns and trends in the market.
- Growth investors focus on earnings and look for fairly-priced companies with the best growth potential as a result.
- Value investors look for stocks that are underpriced in relation to their performance and long-term fundamentals.
- Income investors are seeking current income in the form of dividends, interest or other payments.
- A stock's price indicates what the buying public thinks it is worth.
- The two main ways to purchase individual stocks are through brokers and by using direct purchase plans.
- Low-cost DIPS or DRIPS can be a good choice for investors with limited capital.

CHAPTER FOUR

Buying Hens at the Bond Market

Bonds are loanership investments, or essentially IOUs from government entities and corporations. You know generally what return you will get at the time you purchase them and how long it will take to get it, prompting some investors to describe bonds as "boring." Since bonds have historically returned less than stocks, why would you want them in your portfolio? For starters, when the stock market becomes too volatile, bonds can start to look pretty darn good. This is especially true for those nearing retirement age who don't have the time to wait for a stock market that is spiraling downward to start its often slow recovery. No matter what your age, it is risky to put all your eggs in one basket, so bonds can help diversify your portfolio. Their low correlation with other asset classes helps stabilize the value of your portfolio over time.

It may surprise you to know the bond market is much larger than the stock market; in fact, it's the largest securities market in the world. It is the place where borrowers and lenders meet, with bond dealers acting as intermediaries between the two. Some bonds are traded on the New York Stock Exchange, but mostly the bond market is a virtual, *over-the-counter* (OTC) market where dealers trade securities electronically through their communications networks. If you are interested in a new bond, a bond dealer will provide you with a prospectus detailing its terms and rates, as well as the risks involved in its purchase. Bonds that have already been issued are sold in the secondary market. You can buy them individually or through mutual funds and exchange-traded funds. Some bond dealers maintain their own inventories of bonds for resale, while others simply act as intermediaries who buy and sell from other dealers.

Bond Basics

The interest rate for a bond is frequently referred to as the *coupon* rate. This terminology is a holdover from the days when actual paper certificates were issued. Each certificate had a tear-off portion, or coupon, that the bearer redeemed for cash when an interest payment came due. Nowadays, everything is electronic.

Ratings and Risks

If you were to apply for a loan, the first thing any lender would do is check your credit score. Bonds have credit ratings, too. The rating assigned indicates the creditworthiness of the borrowers (bond issuers). For example, AAA ratings indicate the highest quality while high yield or junk bonds earn a BB (or lower) rating. There are three major rating agencies in the United States: Moody's, Standard and Poor's, and Fitch. These watchdogs continually monitor the performance of companies. If a company's financial condition improves, it may be upgraded; conversely, if its financial condition starts to deteriorate, it may be downgraded or placed on a credit watch list. When rating agencies do not agree on the soundness of a company, the result is called a *split rating*.

High grade bonds add diversity to your portfolio, help reduce volatility, and provide a stable, reliable source of income. Sounds like you couldn't lose with high quality bonds, right? Sorry, but no investment is risk-free. If you hold them to maturity, you will receive the full value—unless the borrower is a company that goes bankrupt and defaults on its obligations. This is called *default risk*.

What happens if you buy a bond at an interest rate of five percent and later the prevailing interest rate for similar bonds rises to seven percent? If you hold the bond, you are losing the extra two percent you could have made on a newer investment. If you decide to sell your bond before its maturity date, who is going to buy it when they can buy a new one paying two percent more? You would have to sell your bond at a discount and take a loss. This is *market risk* or *interest rate risk*, and we will look at this as well as a few other potential pitfalls in more detail shortly.

Types of Bonds

There are three main types of bonds:

- *Fixed-rate bonds* have a set interest rate for the life of the bond. Even though bond prices fluctuate on the secondary market, the amount of the interest payments stays the same. These are appropriately called fixed income investments.
- *Floating-rate bonds* aka *variable-rate bonds* aka *floaters* have interest rates that are reset at pre-determined time intervals. Interest rate changes are aligned with a benchmark such as the Treasury bill rate or the prime interest rate. The benchmark interest rate is often called the reference rate.
- *Accrual bonds* accrue; that is, all the interest earned accumulates and is not paid out until the bond matures or comes due. The price you pay for the bond is less than its face value and the difference is what you receive at maturity. Since there are no interest payments made there are no coupons, hence the name *zero coupon bonds*. Even though investors do not receive payments until maturity, income tax has to be paid on the phantom interest that has accrued on zeros held in taxable accounts.

A bond may contain a *call* provision. This gives the issuer the right—but not the obligation—to pay it off early in case a better deal (for them) comes along. Suppose, for example, you buy a ten-year bond paying seven percent interest. A few years after you buy the bond, the interest rate being paid on similar bonds drops to four percent. The bond issuer can then pay you off early so they can issue new bonds at the lower rate. Instead of feeling smug about owning a seven percent investment in a four percent world, you are now stuck shopping for another investment in a market offering lower yields. This is known as *call risk* or *reinvestment risk*. Because call provisions put investors at a disadvantage, bonds that have them usually offer higher yields.

When the shoe is on the other foot and you have the right to cash in a bond before it matures, you have a *put* bond. You "put" the bond back into the hands of the issuer by selling it back to them, and they pay you face value plus the interest earned to that point. These bonds, as you might expect, have a lower yield than bonds without the put provision.

Yields and Pricing

Stocks are quoted by their trading price but the main consideration when buying bonds, in addition to the credit-worthiness of the issuer, is *yield*. The yield is the return you actually earn on your investment expressed as a percentage. It sounds simple, but unfortunately, it isn't. There are different types of yield, and some of the calculations are quite complicated. Before you stop reading and skip to the next chapter, you should know that if you buy bonds through a broker, they will calculate the various yields for you. You can also find yield calculators online at sites such as www.kiplinger.com. No matter how you get your figures, there are two types of yield any bond investor must know, so let's talk about them now.

The first is *current yield*. Current yield is the return a bond earns annually expressed as a percentage of the investment and it is a simple calculation. Here is the formula:

$$\text{Current Yield} = \frac{\text{Annual interest amount paid by the bond}}{\text{Price paid for the bond}}$$

For example, Ima Investor owns two fixed-rate bonds. Both have a face value of $1,000 and a coupon (annual interest) rate of eight percent. She paid $1,000 for one but only $900 for the other, and she wants to know the current yield of each. Remember on a fixed-rate bond, the interest payments stay the same, regardless of the price paid. Ima divides the annual interest of $80 (8% of $1,000) by the amounts she paid for the bonds, and finds her current yields are 8 percent and 8.89 percent. Here are her calculations:

Bond #1: $80/$1000 = 8%
Bond #2: $80/$900 = 8.89%

The reason her second bond has a higher yield than the first is because she is getting the same $80 return on an asset for which she paid less.

The second important yield is *yield-to-maturity*, which is the percent you will earn annually if you hold the bond until it matures and you reinvest all the interest at that same rate of return. This calculation takes into account all the interest you receive from the time of purchase until the bond matures, plus any gain or loss if you purchased the bond above or below its face value. This figure, which you can get from the broker, helps you to compare bonds with different interest rates and maturities so you can decide which is a better buy. The pros use yield-to-maturity rather than current yield to price bonds. Using current yield will often give you misleading returns.

> Unfortunately, far too many investors take a trip to the land of bonds without knowing the language.
> —LARRY E. SWEDROE

More Bond Speak

Secured bonds are backed by collateral such as company equipment or financial assets, but *unsecured bonds* are not. Unsecured bonds offer a simple promise to pay off the debt at its maturity date. The amount of money you will receive after the bond matures is referred to as the *face value*, the *par value*, or the *principal*. In order to find out what the real rate of return is, you must deduct the rate of inflation from the interest rate. But what if you don't want to hold the bond until it matures? Then you can sell it. Although often not as liquid, bonds are traded on the open market just like stocks and their prices fluctuate daily. For that reason, face value is usually *not* the price of the bond. When a bond sells at face value, it is said to be sold at par. When a bond sells for more than face value, it is said to be selling at a premium and when it sells below its face value, it is said to be selling at a discount. What affects the price? Glad you asked.

Effect of Interest Rate Changes on Bonds

Interest rates and bonds have an inverse relationship. Here is the nutshell version to commit to memory: *the value of a bond decreases*

INVESTING STARTING FROM SCRATCH

when interest rates rise and increases when interest rates fall. It took me forever to understand this concept, but it is actually fairly simple if you keep in mind yield-to-maturity is the key to bond prices. When interest rates rise or fall, the price of an older bond must adjust to keep its yield in line with new bonds; otherwise, no one would buy it. Here is an example: Ima Investor has a $10,000 fixed-rate bond she bought new that will not mature for three more years. The bond has a coupon (interest) rate of five percent, which means it pays her $500 per year. Currently, similar bonds are selling at a coupon rate of four percent, so a new $10,000 bond will only earn $400 per year. Ima would like to sell her bond at a premium and wants to know how much she can ask for it. To arrive at a price, she must determine the total value in today's dollars of the payments that will be made each year in the future. Here are her calculations:

> The value of a bond decreases when interest rates rise and increases when interest rates fall.

Table 3
Effect of Declining Interest Rate on Bonds

Number of years until maturity:	Year 1	Year 2	Year 3	Total
Annual interest:	$500	$500	$10,500	
Divided by:	1.04 $(1.04)^1$	1.08 $(1.04)^2$	1.12 $(1.04)^3$	
Present value of annual interest:	$480.77	$462.96	$9,375	$10,318.73

Let's break this down line by line:

1. Annual interest: Remember the annual interest of a fixed rate bond doesn't change. Ima's five percent bond will pay its owner $500 interest every year until it matures. In year three, the matured bond will pay $500 interest plus return the initial investment, or $10,500.
2. The annual interest ($500) is divided by a decimal. The whole

number "1" in the decimal represents one earning period, which in this case is one year. The fraction to the right of the decimal point is the current interest rate (four percent) with the number of earning periods factored in. In case you've forgotten your high school math class, to raise to a power just multiply the number by itself the specified number of times. Like this:

$$1.04^2 = 1.04 \times 1.04 = 1.08$$
$$1.04^3 = 1.04 \times 1.04 \times 1.04 = 1.12$$

3. The result of her labor is the value of future interest in today's dollars. The $500 interest that will be paid one year from now is worth $480.77 today and the $500 interest that will be paid two years from now is worth $462.96 today.

Adding across, Ima finds she can sell her $10,000 bond for $10,319—a capital gain of $319. But suppose instead of going down, the interest rate for new bonds has gone up to six percent? Her calculations would look like this:

Table 4
Effect of Increasing Interest Rate on Bonds

Number of years until maturity:	Year 1	Year 2	Year 3	Total
Annual interest:	$500	$500	$10,500	
Divided by:	1.06 $(1.06)^1$	1.12 $(1.06)^2$	1.19 $(1.06)^3$	
Present value of annual interest:	$471.70	$446.43	$8,823.53	$9,741.66

Her bond today is worth only $9,742. Ima may take the loss or she may decide to hold onto her bond for awhile longer. Of course, Ima could save herself all this trouble and simply call her broker for a sales price, but she likes to understand how it all works.

The risk that interest rates will change during the term of a bond is referred to as market risk or interest rate risk. If you have a long-term bond and you hold it until maturity, you may see the real value of your bond in terms of purchasing power eroded by rising prices. This is inflation risk. Now that you've learned to speak the lingo, it's time for a stroll through the market.

Government Bonds

Treasury Notes and Bonds

Often referred to simply as "Treasuries," these are loans made to the United States Government. Treasuries have long been considered the safest investment in the world, because everyone prefers to lend money to someone they are almost certain will pay them back. The trade-off for this safety is a lower rate of return. *Treasury Notes* mature in one to ten years, while *Treasury Bonds* have maturities of more than ten years. Both pay a fixed amount of interest (the coupon rate) every six months.

TIPS or Treasury Inflation-Protected Securities were introduced in the late 1990s. These are designed to protect against inflation by providing a guaranteed return over and above the inflation rate. As you have probably already guessed, the coupon rate is lower to offset this guarantee. If you hold the TIPS until maturity, you receive the face value plus an amount equal to the inflation that has taken place over the life of the bond. During periods of *deflation* (prices drop), the value of the TIPS is adjusted downward, but you are still guaranteed to receive the full face value of the TIPS when it matures. In other words, you will lose your bonus, but not your face value.

The U.S. Treasury sells securities through regularly scheduled public auctions. Most are purchased by primary dealers who then offer them for sale on the secondary market through brokers. Treasuries have a minimum face value of $100 and any amount over that is in $100 increments. You can sell only part of a Treasury as long

> The Federal Reserve System uses the Treasury market to manage inflation in the economy. When it wants to reduce interest rates, it puts money into circulation by buying Treasuries, and when it wants to raise interest rates, it takes money out of circulation by selling them.

as the parcels are in multiples of $100. For example, if you had a $10,000 Treasury, you could sell $3,000 off and retain the rest. You can also use them as collateral for a loan from your broker. All Treasuries issued since 1985 are non-callable, which means your interest rate is guaranteed until maturity. The interest income from Treasuries is subject to federal income tax but exempt from state and local taxes.

> Ninety-five percent of Treasuries are held by institutional investors such as pension funds, mutual funds, and insurance companies.

Buying Direct

For do-it-yourselfers, Treasuries can be purchased directly from the government using the Treasury Direct system. Begin by logging on to www.treasurydirect.gov to set up an account. You will need your Social Security number, driver's license number, checking account number, bank routing number, and an e-mail address. Once that is done, you can buy, sell and manage your account right from your computer. The custodian of your securities is the U.S. Government, so the risk of brokerage firm or custodian bankruptcy goes away. There are no fees for this service, but you will have to maintain your own records.

United States Savings Bonds

Yes, the venerable Savings Bond is still around and still considered to be among the safest investments you can buy. Let's look at some of their features:

- They are fully guaranteed by the U.S. Government.
- They can be purchased in denominations as small as $50 with no fees or commissions added.
- They are not callable.
- Interest payments compound semi-annually and accrue monthly.
- Income earned is state and local income tax free.
- Federal income tax can be deferred until they are redeemed.

You must have a Social Security number to purchase U.S. Savings Bonds, but you don't have to live in the United States. Unlike other investments, Savings Bonds cannot be sold to anyone

INVESTING STARTING FROM SCRATCH

else or used as collateral for a loan. They can, however, be passed on to heirs and they can be purchased jointly. Savings Bonds come in two forms, Series EE and Series I.

Series EE Savings Bonds are accrual bonds, which means the interest accumulates and is not paid out until the bonds mature. You can purchase paper Savings Bonds from most banks or through payroll deduction plans if your employer offers that option. Individuals can also purchase electronic Series EE bonds directly from the government at Treasury Direct. There are some differences between the paper and electronic bonds and the rules governing them vary according to the date they were issued—nothing associated with the government is ever uncomplicated. If you are the owner of some issued before April, 2005, you can check the rules governing them on www.treasurydirect.gov, but to keep it simple, we're going to assume you are buying a new Series EE savings bond.

Paper Series EE bonds are like zero coupon bonds—you purchase them at a discount which, in this case, is half the face value. Paper EE bonds are available in denominations of $50, $75, $100, $200, $500, $1,000, $5,000 and $10,000, and there is a $5,000 maximum purchase per person in any one year (a $10,000 face value).

Electronic Series EE bonds are not sold at a discount; they are sold at face value. You can buy them in any amount from the minimum of $25, to the maximum of $5,000, to the penny in any one calendar year. To the penny means if for some reason you wanted to, you could purchase a Series EE bond for say, $100.27.

Both paper and electronic Series EE bonds earn a fixed rate of interest (determined by the issue date) which compounds semi-annually. The Treasury Department guarantees they will double in value in a maximum of twenty years. You can redeem Series EE bonds as soon as six months after purchase, but it will cost you a penalty equal to the last three months' interest. If you hold them for five years or longer, you can redeem Series EE bonds without penalty. They continue to earn interest up to thirty years from their date of purchase, although the fixed rate of interest only applies for twenty years.

Similar to TIPS, Series I Savings Bonds are indexed for inflation. They are sold at face value at a fixed rate of interest, which is adjusted for inflation every six months. New fixed rates and inflation rates are announced each May and November. Interest accrues over the thirty-year life of the bond and is paid upon redemption. The U.S. Treasury calculates the final yield from this bond by combining the fixed rate of return set when you bought the bond with a variable semiannual inflation rate.

Series I bonds come in paper or electronic versions, and the same purchase denominations and rules apply as with Series EE bonds. You can redeem them after one year, but you will forfeit the most recent three months' interest. After five years, you can redeem Series I Savings Bonds without penalty.

Municipal Bonds

"Munis," as they are often called, are issued by municipalities such as cities, states, counties, school districts, airport districts, hospital districts—the list goes on and on—to fund public works. As far as Wall Street is concerned, municipalities are defined as any governing bodies that are not federal. There are two categories of municipal bonds:

- *General obligation bonds* are issued for projects that benefit the entire community such as schools, parks, and road construction. These are repaid by tax revenues, so they have to be approved by the taxpayers in public referendums before they can be issued.
- *Revenue bonds* raise funds to build specific projects, such as toll roads and athletic stadiums. These bonds are repaid by the income earned from the people who use the roads and facilities, and do not require voter approval to be issued.

Tax-exempt municipal bonds are exempt from federal income taxes and sometimes from state and local taxes, too. These have wide appeal to investors in high tax brackets, but because of the tax savings, the yield is usually lower than some other bond choices. Some private projects are not eligible for the federal tax exemptions, so there are also taxable munis. Be sure you understand all the tax implications before buying these.

We have reached the end of the government aisle, but right next to it, we find *government agency bonds* for sale.

Government Agency Bonds

These bonds are issued by major federally-owned or federally-sponsored agencies. You may see the latter referred to as *GSEs*, which is an acronym for "government-sponsored enterprises." Notice the key word "sponsored." Although the U.S. Government does not explicitly guarantee these bonds, many investors believe there is an implied guarantee Uncle Sam will not let them default. There are a number of GSEs, but the largest issuers of bonds by far have names that are familiar to you: They are Fannie Mae, Ginnie Mae, and Freddie Mac, and all of them are in the housing business.

Mortgage-backed securities

For most of us, the first step in buying a home is to obtain a mortgage loan. You go to your chosen lender and fill out an application. After you prove your creditworthiness, pay some fees and sign about a million documents promising to repay them, they usually grant your request. Have you ever wished you could reverse the situation and be the lender for a change? With *mortgage-backed securities* (MBS), you can do just that. Here's how they work:

Most lenders do not wait twenty to thirty years to recover the money they loan on mortgages. Instead, they sell their mortgages to other entities so they can recapture the funds they need to continue making loans. The largest buyers of these debt instruments are Fannie Mae, Ginnie Mae and Freddie Mac. After these agencies check the loans for creditworthiness, they convert them into mortgage securities or "securitize" them. Similar securities are combined to form pools of mortgages. The GSE sells shares of the pool to investors by issuing mortgage-backed securities. Mortgage-backed securities from Fannie Mae, Ginnie Mae and Freddie Mac are considered very safe because the trio guarantees payment to investors, whether or not there is sufficient cash flow into the mortgage pool. It is important to note the guarantees of Fannie Mae and Freddie Mac are not explicitly backed by the U.S. government. They are based on their own corporate well-being and therein lies the risk.*

---

* In the midst of a mortgage meltdown in the U.S., the federal government seized Fannie Mae and Freddie Mac in September 2008 and replaced their directors. Some in the financial world think they should remain under federal control while others favor privatization or even elimination of these agencies. Their fate will be decided by the end of 2009.

I think it might help to understand why these agencies were created. Until the late 1930s, people who wanted to buy homes were required to make down payments of a whopping forty percent, and then pay off the mortgage in only three to five years. They paid only interest on the loan during this period, and then the entire balance was due at the end of the term in a "balloon" payment. When the stock market crashed in 1929, followed by a deep economic depression, many people could not make their payments. The default rate for mortgages went up—about as high as those balloons. The government stepped in and created the Federal National Mortgage Association (FNMA) in 1938 to alleviate the problem. At first, FNMA only bought mortgages issued to lower- income people, but that changed later as banks saw the advantages of making loans. In 1968, the government split the FNMA in two; one part became the privately-managed, shareholder-owned corporation now known as Fannie Mae. Although it is a private company, Fannie Mae operates under the rules of its congressional charter and government agencies provide oversight.

The second part was created within the U.S. Department of Housing and Urban Development (HUD) and named the Government National Mortgage Association, or Ginnie Mae (GNMA). It exists to guarantee mortgages for low to moderate-income homebuyers. The government still owns Ginnie Mae, so the Federal Housing Administration (FHA), the Veteran's Administration (VA), or other government entities insure all mortgages inside its pool.

In 1970, the government waded a little farther into the mortgage pools when it chartered the Federal Home Loan Mortgage Corporation (FHLMC). In 1989, this corporation became a shareholder-owned, privately-managed entity known now as Freddie Mac (FRE). That's the history—now, back to the good part about being the bank...

The mortgage pool receives principal and interest payments from its borrowers—the homeowners. When you own a share in that pool, i.e. mortgage-backed securities, you usually receive a monthly payment representing your share. Remember, this happens whether or not the homeowners make payments, thus the benefit of the guarantee mentioned earlier. You can buy mortgage-backed securities directly from the issuers or, more commonly, through mutual funds because of the large minimum investment required. You may hear mortgage-backed securities referred to as *pass-through securities* because the lenders withhold a small fee before passing the homeowners' payments on to investors.

Risks of Investing in Mortgage-Backed Securities

Safe as they may sound, you know by now there is no such thing as a risk-free investment. Here are three of the predominant risks with this particular type:

1. Prepayment risk. Often homeowners pay their mortgages off early by making extra principal payments or refinancing if interest rates drop. This has a big impact on the pool's yield and lifespan. The unpredictability of future interest rates makes it difficult to compare the yield of a mortgage-backed security to other types of bonds.
2. Interest-rate risk. If interest rates go up instead of down, homeowners will hold onto their mortgages longer and the life of your investment goes on longer than planned. This means you have less money available to put into other investments at a time when interest rates are high.
3. Market risk. If you want to sell your agency bonds before they mature, you face the risk of price changes just like you do with other bonds and stocks.

Other Types of Government Agency Bonds

The Great Depression that began with the stock market crash in 1929 resulted in a wave of bank failures in the United States and a crushing loss of public confidence in our financial structure. In response, Congress established the Federal Home Loan Bank System in 1932 to ensure a steady supply of funds to institutions making consumer home loans. In short, the Federal Home Loan Bank System's main function is to be a lender to the lenders by making low-cost advances to them. The FHL Bank System gets the money for these advances by selling notes and bonds to investors.

The system consists of twelve regional banks located across the country. Originally, their loan activities were confined to savings and loans institutions and some insurance companies. Today, according to the Federal Home Loan Bank System website, their members provide credit reserves to approximately eighty percent of the nation's financial institutions. It has the distinction of being one of the few—if not only—government-related institutions without an acronym or a nickname.

There are more GSEs that issue agency bonds, but *Forbes Magazine* reports the ones we've discussed make up over ninety percent of total agency debt outstanding, so these are the ones you are most likely to come across. This discussion is just a general overview. If you get into bonds and want to learn more, I have included several good resources and websites in Appendix II. Let's move on to the private sector of the market.

Corporate Bonds

Corporate bonds provide a way for companies to raise operating capital if they don't want to issue stock. You, the bond buyer, become the lender and they, the borrowers, pay a stated rate of interest until the due date when they repay the loan. Corporate bonds are most often issued in multiples of $1,000 and $5,000. The terms of these bonds are dictated by the market, but usually short-term means less than five years, intermediate means between five and twelve years, and long term is more than twelve years.

Corporate bonds yield more than Treasuries because there is greater risk involved. Most corporate bonds are *debentures*, which means they are not secured by any specific assets. It is very important to check their ratings carefully—and not just when you buy them. Keep an eye out for ratings changes the entire time you own them. It is important to understand the bond's terms completely. Most corporate bonds have fixed rates of interest, but there are also accrual and floating rate corporate bonds as well as zeros and callable issues. Unlike stock, a bond gives you no ownership in the business; however, in the event of financial trouble, bondholders are paid before stockholders and have a higher claim to the assets of the corporation in cases of bankruptcy or liquidation.

Corporate Retail Notes

Corporate retail notes are fixed-rate, unsecured debts purchased at par directly from the issuing company—well, almost directly. You have to buy them through a broker, but there are usually no additional fees attached. They are issued in $1,000 increments and most are callable. These notes have a variety of coupon rates and terms and are offered weekly. Corporate retail notes are designed to be held until maturity so there is not much of a secondary market for them. Large, highly-rated corporations usually issue these notes and they are suitable for laddering (coming up in the last section of this chapter). For more info, see www.internotes.com.

Junk Bonds

Junk bonds are just what their name implies. They are issued by companies who have low credit ratings or are otherwise on shaky financial ground, so they have to pay a higher rate of interest to get people to take a chance on them. Sometimes new start-up companies who have no credit rating issue these bonds, but more often the issuing companies have high debt or are otherwise distressed. There has been quite a bit of scandal attached to junk bonds, so you may see them euphemistically referred to as *high yield bonds* instead, just as a used car is now called "pre-owned." Two other terms associated with junk bonds you might see are these:

- *Fallen Angels* are bonds that were once investment grade but were downgraded when the issuing company fell on hard times.
- *Rising Stars* are bonds whose status is improving with the issuing company's credit rating. These may eventually become investment quality.

A number of mutual funds specialize in junk bonds. The idea is that their portfolio managers are able to judge the credit quality of the bond issuers and that wide diversification protects against the default of a few issuers. Some speculators have earned fortunes from trading junk bonds—a few others have earned prison terms. Junk bonds are not for beginning investors, and even when you feel bolder, don't bet your egg farm on them.

Convertible Bonds

Convertibles are bonds that can be converted into common stock at a pre-set conversion ratio. Unlike other bonds, they provide the opportunity for significant price appreciation if the issuing companies stock rises significantly. Most of them are issued by smaller, speculative companies or companies with high debt or unstable earnings that cannot easily obtain financing any other way. In addition, they are almost always callable. If you want to dabble in these, I recommend you wait until you are an experienced investor.

Asset-Backed Bonds

These are relatively new items in the bond marketplace. Just like the mortgage-backed securities we discussed earlier, these are shares in pools of other types of debt such as credit cards, auto loans, and accounts receivable. Institutions who buy loans from banks and other lenders create the pools.

Making a Purchase

In the secondary market, prices are quoted in $100 increments regardless of the bond's face value. For example, a bond quoted at ninety-six is a bond priced at $96 per $100 of face value, which means it is discounted four percent. Here's the formula to calculate the percentage of discount:

$$\frac{\text{Face value} - \text{price}}{\text{Face value}} \text{ or } \frac{\$100 - \$96}{\$100} = \frac{\$4}{\$100} = .04 \text{ or } 4\%$$

Generally, bond dealers do not operate on commission like stockbrokers. Instead, they operate like retailers who make their profit by marking up the wholesale price. Since dealers set their own prices (within regulatory guidelines), it is important to shop around. A good website to help you compare prices is www.investinginbonds.com. This site also contains some excellent tutorials on bond investing in general.

Bond mutual funds allow you to own a wider array of bonds than you could probably afford on your own, which means broader risk diversity. There are myriad types of funds—taxable, tax-exempt, municipal bonds, corporate bonds, high-yield bonds, MBS funds and on and on. These funds have professional managers who, of course, are not free. Be sure and consider all fees when you are contemplating buying into a fund, including both "front-end loads" upon purchase and the annual management fee. Also, check the fund's Morningstar rating. (We will get to these in Chapter 7). Since a fund owns a variety of bonds, it contains no one specific maturity date, which means the value of the fund changes from day to day. This makes it impossible to calculate yield-to-maturity.

Bond unit investment trusts (UITs) have a different twist. A selection of bonds is held in a fixed portfolio until the last one matures. This gives you the benefit of knowing exactly how much you will earn while you are invested in the fund. Since there are no changes—unless one of the bonds defaults or is called—there are usually no management fees attached to these, but check for sales fees, which can be quite high.

Bonds are entirely different types of investments from stocks. If you decide to add them to your portfolio, it is vital the broker you select is well-versed in their intricacies. Here are a few ideas to help you find a good bond brokerage firm:

- Ask for recommendations from friends and family.
- Check your candidates to see if they are members of the Securities Investor Protection Corporation (SIPC), which will help protect you if the firm goes bankrupt.
- Ask your prospective brokerage firm what types of bonds they specialize in and how they are paid.
- Interview prospective brokers. Ask how much experience she has. Does her philosophy jibe with yours? Can she help you achieve your investment objectives?
- If possible, talk to some of the firm's existing clients.
- Call (800) 289-9999 for a background check of your dealer. This is a toll-free number maintained by the SEC and operated by FINRA.
- Beware of any investment professional who does not listen to you or who tries to push you into investments you are unsure of.

Investment Strategies for Individual Bonds

If you like the idea of purchasing individual bonds, a popular technique to help minimize interest rate risk is called *laddering*. You

Buying Hens at the Bond Market

build your ladder by purchasing securities with various maturity dates. Each bond represents a rung, and the height of the ladder is determined by the distance between the rungs created by the different maturity dates. Here is an example:

Ima has $25,000 she wants to invest in individual bonds. She decides to build her ladder by purchasing five bonds. Each bond has a face value of $5,000, but the interest rates vary because their terms are different. She staggers her maturity dates two years apart. The first bond (A) will mature in two years, bond B in four years, bond C in six years, bond D in eight years, and bond E will reach maturity in ten years.

Table 5
Ima's Ten Year Bond Ladder

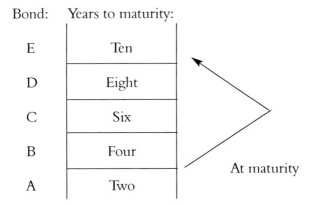

Because Ima is saving for retirement and does not need the income now, when bond A matures, she will use the proceeds to buy another ten-year bond and keep her ladder going. Using this technique, Ima will be able to take advantage of rising interest rates in a bull market and minimize her losses in a bear bond market. Later, when she retires, she can use this strategy to provide a predictable, steady source of income as each bond matures.

Another way to minimize risk is to buy bonds with maturities at both ends of the spectrum. Instead of distributing your risk evenly over a period of time as with laddering, you would buy half short-term and half long-term instruments. This is called the *barbell* technique.

THE BOTTOM LINE

- Bonds are loans to governments, government entities and corporations.
- There are three main types of bonds: fixed rate, floating rate and accrual.
- Bond can be short-term, intermediate-term or long-term.
- The main considerations when buying bonds are yield-to-maturity and the creditworthiness of the issuer.
- When the bond price goes up, yield goes down.
- When the bond price goes down, yield goes up.
- Interest rates and bond prices have an inverse relationship: when rates go up, bond prices go down and vice versa.
- U.S. government bonds are considered the safest investment in the world.
- Municipal bonds are usually tax exempt.
- GSE bonds have an implied guarantee by the U.S. government.
- Corporate bonds have a higher yield because the risks are higher than with government bonds.
- Junk bonds are also known as high yield bonds.
- Bonds can be purchased individually or through mutual funds.
- Laddering and barbell techniques can be used to decrease risk.
- The main risks associated with bonds are default risk, market risk, inflation risk and early call risk.

CHAPTER FIVE

Buying Hens at the Money Market

THE MONEY MARKET is a member of the fixed income family and a close cousin of the bond market. The offerings here are debt securities, but usually for very short terms—anywhere from one day to one year. It is where large financial institutions, major corporations, and governments lend and borrow from each other to manage their temporary cash flow needs. Sums high enough to boggle the mind change hands here every day, but there are also some shopping opportunities for egg farmers.

Why Shop Here?

Here are some of the reasons you might want to make purchases in this market:

- The money market is a good place to keep your emergency funds or funds for a large expense you know is coming up. Investments here are highly liquid and earn interest until you withdraw them.
- You have capital to invest but have not yet decided what to buy. You can think of it as a sort of "gym" for your cash where it can put on a little interest muscle while you are idling or doing your research.
- You need a refuge when the stock market is too volatile or a bear market comes along.

Buying Hens at the Money Market

- When interest rates are rising, money market returns are more attractive.
- Safety is your paramount concern.

Like the bond market, the money market has no actual physical exchange, so all trades are completed electronically or by phone. These loanership investments are extremely safe but they also offer the lowest returns. Alas, you cannot have it both ways.

> **Money is better than poverty if only for financial reasons.**
> —Woody Allen

What You Can Buy at the Money Market

Treasury Bills

Treasury bills (commonly called T-bills) are debt instruments issued by the U.S. treasury that mature in one year or less. The most common terms are four-, thirteen-, or twenty-six weeks, and the minimum purchase amount is $100.

Here is how they work: Each week, on Monday and Tuesday, the treasury auctions T-bills below par (at a discount), so the difference between the face value and the sales price is the gain. The discount rate set at the time the bill is auctioned determines the amount of interest that is paid when the bill matures—no interest is paid prior to maturity. Auction purchases require bidding, and you can bid on T-bills two ways:

1. Competitive bidders set the lowest discount rate they will accept, which means they will not always "win" the bill they want. Banks, brokers, and dealers fulfill purchases made by competitive bidders. These entities do not earn commissions on trades but operate instead as wholesalers, buying and selling securities from their own accounts.
2. Non-competitive bidders simply accept whatever discount rate the auction determines. Although you cannot know in advance exactly what the interest rate will be, you do know you will buy something that day. Non-competitive bidders can buy T-bills through brokers and dealers or directly from the government using the Treasury Direct system. (See Chapter Four for instructions on how to set up an account). After you

INVESTING STARTING FROM SCRATCH

have opened your account, just enter the amount you want to invest and the date you want to buy and your transaction will be completed at the next auction. You can even set up recurring purchases for up to five years if you want. Only non-competitive bidders can use the Treasury Direct system.

Like bonds, the thing that interests investors the most is the yield they earn on these investments. Calculating the yield on a T-bill employs this fairly simple formula:

$$\frac{\text{Face value} - \text{price paid}}{\text{Price paid}} \times \frac{365}{\text{Days to maturity}}$$

Let's look at an example. Ima Investor pays $990 for a $1,000 T-bill with a term of thirteen weeks, which means she will have a gain of $10 when it matures. To calculate her yield, she uses the formula shown above. Here are her calculations:

$10/$990 = 0.0101 × 365/91 = 4.010

(13 weeks × 7 days)

($1,000 $− 990)

or

0.0101 × 4.010 = 0.0405

To convert this number to a percentage, she simply moves the decimal point two places to the right and finds the yield on her T-bill was 4.05 percent.

You can sell your T-bills before they mature, but you may suffer some losses if you do. T-bills are popular because they are short-term, affordable to the individual investor, and exempt from state and local taxes. They are widely considered to be the safest investment in the world if held to maturity.

Certificate of Deposit

A *certificate of deposit* (or CD) is a savings certificate that typically entitles you to receive a fixed rate of interest at the end of a specified

Buying Hens at the Money Market

term. CDs are *time deposits*, which means you cannot draw upon them until the term has expired without paying a substantial penalty. The most common terms are between one month and five years, but there are other lengths of time available. When the CD matures, you get your principal back along with the interest earned or, if you wish, you can renew it for another term. Banks are the most common sellers of CDs, but you can also buy them from brokers and other salespeople. CDs purchased from brokers can be bought and sold in the secondary market, which means there are no penalties if you sell them prior to maturity. They are, of course, subject to market risk like any other investment. Bank-issued CDs have the added safety feature of being insured by the FDIC up to $100,000.* Although deposit brokers may offer bank-issued CDs, many brokered CDs are not insured by the FDIC.

At one time, these products were fairly straightforward, but some new variations have emerged in our competitive investment marketplace that can be a little tricky. For example, some institutions offer variable rate CDs which have interest rates that change over time. Some have interest rates tied to an index; others contain "steps" with pre-set conditions determining how the rates will change. CDs with a call feature allow the issuer to call the CD (cash you out) after a specified period of time if interest rates change significantly—in their favor.

It is imperative you thoroughly understand what you are buying before you hand over your money. Read everything, assume nothing, and get it all in writing. Here are some things to check out:

1. Is the interest rate fixed or variable?
2. What is the exact date of maturity? What happens at that time? Is there an automatic renewal provision in the contract?
3. Are there call features?
4. What are the penalties for early withdrawal?
5. Is the CD insured by the FDIC?
6. If you are not buying from a bank, check out the deposit broker carefully by calling your state securities regulator. Is there any history of com-

> **Read everything, assume nothing, and get it all in writing.**

---

* At the end of 2008, Congress passed legislation which would temporarily allow the FDIC to insure non-retirement bank deposits for up to $250,000 through effective through December 31, 2009.

plaints? You can also research individual brokers online at www.finra.org.

An important thing to understand when buying a CD is the difference between *annual percentage rate* (APR) and *annual percentage yield* (APY). APR is simply the annual rate of interest paid without taking compounding into account. When an investment pays interest annually, APY and APR are the same, but when interest is paid more frequently, the APY gets higher because interest starts accumulating on interest, or compounding. Through the magic of compounding, the more frequently interest is calculated, the more you will make. Make sure you are comparing apples to apples when considering CDs for purchase.

For example, Ima Investor has $1,000 to tuck away, and she is comparison shopping for CDs. Bank A is offering a one-year, fixed rate CD that compounds monthly and pays an APR of 5.17 percent. Bank B is advertising a one-year, fixed rate CD that compounds quarterly and has an APY of 5.29 percent. What formula does she use to determine the better deal? It's simple—she doesn't. Ima just calls Bank A and asks for the APY. She knows better than to waste her time trying to do complicated equations when someone else has already done the work for her. Alternatively, she can plug the numbers into an online calculator such as the one found on www.bankrate.com and find the answer herself. This site, incidentally, is also a good place for her to do her comparison shopping. So which is the better deal? Bank B's offer sounds better, but Ima learns the APY at Bank A is also 5.29 percent. Perhaps Bank A should consider hiring a new ad agency.

Commercial Paper

Commercial paper is a type of unsecured promissory note issued by large corporations, utilities, finance companies and other industries. Bypassing banks provides a quicker and more cost-effective way for these businesses to borrow money for their short-term needs.

After the stock market crashed in 1929, Congress passed the Securities Act of 1933 which requires all securities offered for sale to the public to be registered with the SEC. Before this law, companies did not have to disclose sales and earnings figures and probably no one had even heard of a prospectus. As seems to frequently be the case, there are some exceptions built into these rules, and commercial paper is designed to take advantage of them. Commercial paper is exempt from the SEC registration requirement if it meets these guidelines:

- The maturity date must be less than 270 days from the date of issue. This is why terms are almost always less than nine months, with one or two months being the average.
- Funds must only be used to finance current operations, such as purchasing inventory, and not for fixed assets on a permanent basis. For example, this means a company could not build a new plant and then use these instruments as a financing source to pay for it.

Like Treasury Bills, commercial paper is issued at a discount, so the difference between face value and the price paid at maturity equals the investment return. Since this type of loan is not backed by any type of collateral, it is typically issued only by companies with excellent credit ratings that are able to attract investors because of the low risk of default. Independent rating companies, such as Moody's and Standard and Poor's, rate issuers of commercial paper for creditworthiness.

Large entities need large sums to operate. Commercial paper denominations are usually $100,000 or more, so most individual investors purchase it only within mutual funds. The yields are higher than T-bills, and about the same as interest rates paid on *Jumbo CDs*, which are certificates of deposit that generally have minimums of $100,000.

Bankers' Acceptances

Bankers' acceptances are short-term credit instruments guaranteed by a bank and usually used to fund international trade. Suppose, for example, an American corporation wants to import goods from a company in China, but the Chinese company doesn't have a prior business history with them and will not extend credit. The Chinese want to be paid when they ship the goods, but the Americans want terms—buy now and pay later. To resolve the impasse, the Americans bring in a third party and use acceptance financing. Here's how it works:

The American buyers go to their bankers, with whom they have a good credit relationship, and draw up an acceptance contract. In this contract, the bank agrees to accept *time drafts* from the American company. A time draft is like a post-dated check or an IOU with a predetermined payment date, usually no longer than 180 days from the date it's written. The bank gives the amount of the time draft, less a percentage (discount), to the Americans—in effect, the bank "cashes" the post-dated check—and the Americans use these funds to pay the Chinese. The Americans get their terms, the Chinese get their payment and the bank earns a fee for their service—everybody is happy.

At the time the bank accepts a time draft, the responsible bank officer stamps the draft "accepted" and the debt becomes the bank's obligation. The bank has become a substitute creditor for its clients—the American company—by guaranteeing to pay the note when it matures. The bank can hold the draft until it matures or get immediate cash by selling it on the secondary market at a discount, or below face value. When the maturity date rolls around, the American corporation pays off its IOU to the bank, and the bank pays the face value of the bankers' acceptance to the investor. In a nutshell, bankers' acceptances are short-term IOUs guaranteed by an intermediary. Like T-bills, the difference between the amount paid and the face value is the return on the investment.

> Banker's acceptances were in use as early as the 12th Century to finance trade.

Eurodollars

Eurodollars are often confused with the currency, euros, but one actually has nothing to do with the other. Eurodollars are American dollars deposited at banks located outside the United States, often as a result of international trade. They are called eurodollars because this market originated in Europe, but now deposits may be found in banks around the globe.

These funds are not subject to U.S. banking regulations, which means banks have more latitude to operate and can make loans with narrower margins. Most eurodollars are held in time deposits and certificates of deposit that offer attractive interest rates to investors. The average eurodollar deposit is in the millions, so the only way for individuals to invest in these is through money market mutual funds.

Repurchase Agreements

Repurchase agreements (repos for short), are frequently used for overnight borrowing between the major players in the money mar-

Buying Hens at the Money Market

ket. The borrower uses securities, usually T-bills, as collateral for a loan with the agreement that the borrower will buy the securities back again at a later date for a specific price. In other words, this is a secured loan with a twist. The entity that sells and then repurchases the securities performs a "repo"; the entity that buys and then resells the security performs a "reverse repo." The difference between the sale price and the cost of repurchasing the security is the interest paid for the loan.

> The importance of money flows from it being a link between the present and the future.
> —John Maynard Keynes

Making a Purchase

Because of the huge minimum investments required, most of us will trade in the money market through mutual funds sold through brokerages and mutual fund companies. Some funds hold only one type of money market instrument and others are composed of a variety. No matter what the holdings, the SEC requires the average maturity date in a money market mutual fund be less than ninety days. There are even some tax-free funds of short-term debt issued by tax-exempt state and local governments. Tax-free may be music to your ears, but you should know these funds generally produce lower returns. A qualified financial professional familiar with your tax situation is your best source of advice about whether or not these may be right for you.

Money market mutual funds add diversity and liquidity to your portfolio and many professionals consider them the best place to keep your emergency reserves. Some advisors recommend keeping as little as three to six months of living expenses here and others recommend keeping up to three years' worth. This is because the historical average downturn of the stock market lasts three years, and the extra margin of safety will protect against having to sell stock at a low point. Although money market mutual funds are very safe, they are not insured by the FDIC or anyone else, and you can lose money investing in them. As with all investment products, you should comparison shop, check the fees, and read each prospectus. Money market mutual funds provide returns that are only marginally better than you can get in a regular savings account. They will not pave your road to riches, but they can provide a nice place to step off of it while you regroup and catch your breath.

> Money market mutual funds are regulated by the SEC and should not be confused with money market accounts, which are completely different. A money market account is a savings account that you open at a bank or credit union. They differ from regular savings accounts in that they have higher minimum balance requirements and pay higher rates of interest. Like any other bank account, money market accounts are insured by the FDIC up to a limit of $100,000. Money market mutual funds are not guaranteed by the FDIC (or anyone else.)

THE BOTTOM LINE

- Money market securities generally mature in less than one year.
- Treasury Bills are considered the safest investment in the world.
- A CD, or certificate of deposit, is a time deposit that may have significant penalties for early withdrawal.
- APY (annual percentage yield) takes compound interest into account; APR (annual percentage rate) does not.
- Commercial paper is a type of unsecured promissory note issued by large corporations, utilities, finance companies and other industries.
- Bankers' acceptances are short-term credit instruments guaranteed by a bank and usually associated with foreign trade.
- Eurodollars are American dollars deposited at banks outside the United States and usually held in time deposits.
- Repurchase agreements are overnight, secured loans that use government securities as collateral.
- Most individual investors participate in the money market through mutual funds.
- Money market securities are liquid and safe, but pay lower returns than other types of investments.
- Money market mutual funds should not be confused with money market accounts offered by banks and credit unions.

CHAPTER SIX

Buying Hens at the Real Estate Market

BOOKSTORE SHELVES ARE CROWDED with titles promising to teach you how to get rich by investing in real estate. Have you ever fantasized what it would be like to own your own office building? How about some apartments, or even a shopping mall? "Dream on," you may be thinking, "that would be impossible for someone in my income bracket." What if I told you it is not only possible, it is relatively easy to accomplish? Okay, maybe you can't buy an entire property, but you can own part of one—or even part of hundreds—and it is as simple as buying stocks. Golden egg farmer, meet the REIT hens.

> The best investment on Earth is earth.
> —Louis Glickman

What Are REITs?

In 1960, Congress passed legislation creating *Real Estate Investment Trusts*, or REITs (pronounced "reets") to level the real estate playing field for average investors. REITs are unique in that they can be both ownership (equity) and loanership (debt) investments. REITs offer a variety of investment options, but there are two general categories:

Equity REITs make up more than ninety percent of the market, so when you hear people talk about REITs, they are usually referring to this type. These special holding companies own and manage pools of

Investments and Financial Services

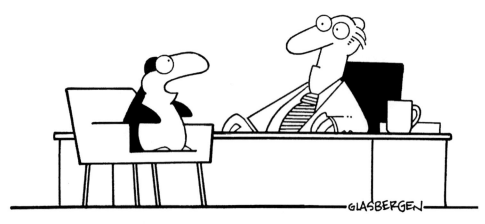

"I have 30,000 fish saved for my retirement. I'd like to roll them over into something that doesn't stink to high heaven!"

income-producing properties. Investors buy shares of the pool, in effect becoming co-owners of the properties held. Equity REITs provide individuals with a way to invest in large-scale commercial properties—something that would be impossible for most of us to do on our own. Their main source of income is rent from leases and fees collected from tenants for other direct services. They may also buy, renovate, sell or develop properties in the course of their business.

Mortgage REITs loan money to buyers of real estate or purchase existing mortgages or mortgage-backed securities. Their source of income is interest from mortgage loans. You generally find these offered by companies that use sophisticated hedging and finance techniques. (We will talk about hedging strategies in Chapter Eight). Mortgage REITs account for less than ten percent of the market.

You may see the terms UPREIT (short for Umbrella Partnership REIT) and DownREIT, but these are just terms explaining how the REIT was formed for tax purposes and not something that concerns investors.

Rules of REITs

In order for a company to qualify as a REIT, it must strictly follow certain IRS guidelines. This is not a complete list, but it covers the major rules:

- It must be managed by a board of directors or trustees.
- It must invest at least seventy-five percent of its total assets in real estate.
- At least seventy-five percent of its income must come from real estate activities in the form of rents or interest on mortgages.
- It must have fully transferable shares and a minimum of 100 shareholders.
- No more than fifty percent of its shares can be owned by five or fewer individuals during the last half of the taxable year.
- It must pay out at least ninety percent of its annual taxable income to its shareholders in the form of dividends.

The last item on the list is the reason REITs are so attractive to investors. You may be wondering what's in it for the company if they distribute all that money to their shareholders. One benefit is the company gets to deduct the dividends from its taxable income, which means REITs rarely pay corporate income tax and, in most cases, no state income tax either. Instead, the shareholders pay the taxes on dividends and *capital gains*. Another reason the company is pleased to distribute earnings is that the managers are usually also investors.

Learning Your Way Around the Market

You can buy REITs two different ways:

1. Publicly-traded REITs have shares that trade easily, just like other stocks. In fact, you may hear them referred to as "real estate stocks." They appear on every exchange, but you will find the majority listed on the New York Stock Exchange. There are close to 200 of these in the United States as of 2008, valued at more than $475 billion. Publicly-traded REITs are required to file financial and operating reports with the SEC on a regular basis and they must follow the same SEC rules as all other public companies. They are widely tracked in the financial world, so information on them is readily available.
2. As their name implies, non-exchange-traded REITs are not traded on the national stock exchanges, although they do file reports with the SEC. Some investors like non-exchange-traded REITs because their share price does not fluctuate daily. Sometimes these are new REITs still acquiring properties that plan to go public in the future. Purchase fees and expenses are usually higher than publicly-traded REITs, as is the minimum investment required. There are not many of these on the market—only about twenty as of this writing.
3. Private REITs are not registered with the SEC and their shares are not traded on the stock exchanges. These are typically sold by financial professionals and the minimum investment requirements are often much higher. The dividend yields are often greater, too, so that can make them appear very attractive; however, before you invest in these, it is important for you to know these are not liquid investments—you cannot sell

them just by calling your broker. In addition, they can have substantial commissions attached and may involve significant management and other fees. There is no outside, independent (read: objective) source of performance information, so it would be wise to postpone investing in them until you are REIT-savvy.

Since we are starting from scratch, we will confine our discussion to publicly-traded equity REITs. They are not only the most common type, but also the simplest way to get started in this market. Equity REITs buy and sell real estate, but they are not in the business of flipping properties. They buy and develop them to hold and operate rather than to resell. Equity REITs own a wide variety of commercial property types and each type of property has its own cycles, idiosyncrasies, quirks, and risk factors. Let's browse around this section of the market.

What You Can Buy at the Equity REIT Market

Apartments
The financial health of the regions where apartments are located has a strong impact on occupancy rates. When the economy is booming, people move into an area to take newly-created jobs and the demand for apartments increases. When industries falter or factories close, these workers lose their jobs and have to move out.

Occupancy is also affected by interest rate fluctuations. High interest rates cause people to postpone buying houses, and apartments prosper. When the rates go down, people begin to think about home ownership, and retaining tenants becomes more difficult.

Office Buildings
An attractive, well-maintained office building in a desirable location can be a wonderful asset to own—unless there are too many of them. Overbuilding is probably the biggest risk factor for this type of real estate. Another is an economic downturn in an area that depends largely on one industry. During the 1980s "oil bust" in Houston, businesses collapsed, jobs evaporated and entire high-rise buildings

stood vacant of tenants. These were called "see-through" buildings because they had so few tenants people joked you could see right through them. (The owners weren't laughing.)

Hotels

Hotel occupancy is strongly tied to the state of the economy and the travel industry. When times are good, people travel for both business and pleasure. When things are a bit leaner, they stick closer to home. Expenses at the hotel continue regardless of whether the rooms are filled or not, so these properties can be severely strained during prolonged downturns. Hotels are also subject to the risk of overbuilding.

Strip Shopping Centers

Most of us love the convenience of shopping at strip centers for necessity items. They are usually anchored by one or two big stores such as a supermarket or a pharmacy. The biggest risk factor in a strip center is the failure or loss of an anchor store. Other risks include location in a deteriorating area, overbuilding, and competition from big box and discount stores.

> Big box stores are huge, freestanding, mega stores. Wal-Mart, Home Depot, and Best Buy are familiar examples.

Malls

Shopping seems to be a national pastime, and malls are in the business of helping us spend our money—mostly on luxury items and entertainment. The health of the economy has a substantial impact on the success of the stores, but since mall owners enjoy long-term leases with their tenants, they are not as sensitive as their retailers to the ups and downs of the economy. Other factors that can make or break a mall are traffic patterns, building trends and the tenant mix. Main competition for malls comes from big-box stores, discount stores, "lifestyle" outdoor shopping centers, catalog shopping and e-commerce.

Industrial Properties

Industrial properties include warehouses and distribution centers which are tied to the flow of goods across the economy. A big advantage to this type of property is it may require only minimal expenditures for the owners to keep it in good repair. It is, after all, a warehouse. The principal risks in this category are overbuilding and declining economic conditions. A relatively small percentage of REITS focus exclusively on industrial properties.

Self-Storage Units

These seem to sprout up like toadstools after a rain as we gather more stuff than our homes and offices will hold. Like industrial properties, they are fairly low-maintenance buildings. The primary risk in this category is overbuilding.

Health Care Facilities

This category includes nursing homes, assisted living properties, hospitals, clinics, and medical office buildings. REITs that hold these facilities in their portfolios of properties do not operate them; they lease them to health-care providers. This type of property is fairly recession proof because the need for these facilities is driven by health-care issues and there is a growing demand for these services as our population ages. The financial stability and integrity of the tenant operators is an important concern, but the biggest risk factor is the way these lessees are paid for their services. Medicare and other government reimbursement programs determine a large part of health care providers' incomes, and these programs can change with the prevailing political winds.

How Investors Make Money with REITs

REITs are moderate-growth, high-dividend investments. When you own any other type of stock, the company's board of directors may or may not authorize payment of a dividend, but REITs must pay them to their shareholders. As previously stated, most of the dividends come from earnings on property leases and payments from tenants for other direct services. When the economy is good, REIT managers can increase rents as leases expire, thus boosting income. Some of the money may come from capital gains if the REIT sells a property during the year, and some may be a return of part of your invested capital. The IRS taxes these types of income at different rates, but REITs furnish a 1099-DIV form at the end of each year that will give you the information you need for tax purposes.

The second way investors make money is through increasing share prices as the values of the properties held by the REIT appreciate. When inflation is high, the properties inside the REIT can become more valuable which, over time, will increase the value of your shares. When the economy is stagnant, the steady earnings from dividends, adjusted for inflation, can help keep your portfolio on an even keel.

REITs add diversity to your portfolio because real estate has historically had a low correlation with both stocks and bonds. That means when one asset class is down, another asset class is up. If you have funds in all of them—and if you have chosen well—somewhere you will probably be making money. Diversity is really all a matter of balance. Statistics indicate as an asset class, REITs' returns are typically somewhat lower than stocks but higher than low-risk bonds.

Remember there is no such thing as a risk-free investment. The same rules of due diligence apply across all asset classes. Like stocks, every REIT comes with SEC-required disclosure documents which the wise investor reads carefully. To understand what you are buying and why, you must do your homework.

Shopping Strategies

Investors employ different strategies to buy REITs just as they do for other kinds of stock. Growth investors look for REITs with earnings growing faster than average. Faster growth may be because the properties are in a boom sector or location, or because management is actively buying or developing properties in a sound economy. Some growth-oriented REITs invest in foreign properties. Value investors are shopping for bargains and looking for undervalued REITs. These REITs may own underperforming properties or have mediocre management, but the value investor believes they are due for a turnaround. Income investors are primarily interested in a safe and relatively high income stream. They buy REITs with modest debt, and stable, reliable dividends.

Finding the Right Price

Like stocks, share prices of REITs increase over time as a company's earnings rise. While stock-pickers look closely at earnings per share (eps), the measure of a REIT's performance is expressed as

Buying Hens at the Real Estate Market

FFO or *funds from operations*. Investors use FFO instead of earnings because of depreciation. This concept is beyond the scope of this book, but here is a nutshell version of what it means:

Real property is subject to *depreciation* for accounting purposes. Depreciation is a measure, established by U.S. tax laws, of the useful life of an asset. This measure can—and does—change as Congress changes tax laws, but currently it is set at thirty-nine years for commercial real estate obtained after May 13, 1993. The countdown starts as soon as the owners make the property available for rental. Each year, at least as far as the IRS is concerned, the building is worth a little less until finally it reaches zero or is, in accounting terms, fully depreciated. Does that mean after thirty-nine years the building is worth nothing? No—in fact, it could be worth a great deal more depending upon its location and condition. The land under the building does not depreciate at all—indeed, it may appreciate in value over time enough to offset the depreciation of the building. It's a tax and accounting thing.

> **Buy land. They ain't making any more of the stuff.**
> —WILL ROGERS

The depreciated value of the REIT's assets, in this case real property, appears on the REIT company's *balance sheet*. (A balance sheet is like a snapshot of a company's net worth at any given point in time.) Since this figure includes depreciation, it is not very meaningful to investors. In order to get an accurate picture of the value of the assets, REIT investors add depreciation expense back in—and that is the concept of FFO.

Location Considerations

Most REITs specialize in one property type. Some own properties in only one region, and others have holdings across the United States as well as in foreign countries. There are pros and cons to each type. A REIT that owns properties in only one area is likely to have very deep roots in the community and may have local, specialized knowledge that can give its managers a competitive edge. On the other hand, REITs that operate properties in many areas of the country have a reduced risk of regional decline. We have all seen times when a major industry tumbles and all the supporting businesses in the area go down with it. Office buildings may stand empty for months—even years—but this is very unlikely to happen at the same time all over the country.

The law of supply and demand will always govern real estate. There are boom and bust cycles—one area of the country may be red hot while in another, you can't give a building away. Real estate is about three things: location, location, location—and REITs are no exception. But REITs are about something else, too: management, management, management.

The Role of Managers

Real estate, at least as owned by today's REITs, is not a passive investment where managers just sit back and wait for rent checks to roll in. The management team of a REIT may be the single most important factor in its success or failure. Even the best properties can flounder under poor leadership. Skilled, effective REIT managers:

- Are always vigilant for opportunities to acquire or develop properties.
- Are open to selling and exchange opportunities.
- Keep up with trends—they know what tenants are looking for and where they are looking for it.
- Keep properties well-maintained and upgraded and offer services that are attractive to tenants. They generate maximum profits for the properties they manage by maintaining high occupancy rates.
- Increase rental rates on a regular basis. Most commercial leases contain clauses that provide for periodic rent increases, usually based on an index of inflation. These are known as rent "bumps" or rent "hikes." In addition, managers of retail properties frequently negotiate percentage rent increases with their tenants. This means if the retailers' sales exceed a specified amount, they pay a certain percentage of the overage as additional rent. Tenants are willing to agree to this when they know the property managers will keep their buildings in tip-top shape, which helps attract shoppers.
- Keep the tenant mix upgraded. Good managers weed out less-desirable tenants as their leases expire and replace them with higher-quality lessees.
- Watch costs like hawks, including corporate overhead. Some use strategies like expense sharing where tenants pay a portion of expenses for maintenance of common areas such as janitor-

> **The very best management teams perform well, even when their tenants do not.**
> —RALPH L. BLOCK

ial, security and energy costs. Many times properties are leased on a triple net basis. A *triple net lease* means the tenant pays for repairs, utilities, and insurance—in other words, just about everything—in addition to the rent.

When considering a REIT, check to see if the managers are also shareholders. If so, they have a direct financial stake in the company's successful performance. This is the same principle as investigating inside ownership of a stock.

Advantages of REITs Over Owning Individual Properties

REITs offer several significant advantages over owning individual properties:

- Simplicity. REITs are the simplest way to invest in real estate.
- Greater diversity. Equity REITs offer investors the opportunity to co-own many types of properties in various parts of the country, or even the world—a feat that would be extremely difficult for any individual to accomplish on her own.
- Greater liquidity. When you own individual real estate, rarely can you sell it immediately, nor can you sell just a few rooms and keep the rest. You can buy or sell a publicly-traded REIT easily, and you never have to wonder if you got a fair price, because its value is updated daily via the stock market.
- Professional management. Late night infomercials tout the fortunes that can be made in real estate. What they fail to mention is the back-breaking labor, the nights and weekends waiting for prospective tenants to show up, and the drudgery of cleaning up the debris from other peoples' lives. Here is one more thing to consider: If investing in individual properties is as lucrative as the gurus say, why aren't they out buying property instead of making money selling books and tapes?

> Sometimes the people who make serious money in real estate are the people who tell you how to make serious money in real estate.

How To Make a Purchase

You can buy shares of publicly-traded REITs through a stockbroker, a discount brokerage firm or by contacting the REIT directly. Many REITs offer DRIPS, or dividend reinvestment plans. There are also more than seventy REIT mutual funds. Mutual funds can provide excellent diversification since most of them own at least thirty different REITs, but since most of them are actively managed, they can also come with some hefty commission and management fees. If you want to keep fees down, REIT index funds and exchange-traded funds are other options. If you choose to make a purchase through a broker, make sure she is well-versed in this type of investment.

Are REITS Good Investments?

Equity REITs are subject to the same factors that can negatively affect any other type of real estate investment. Economic downturns, poor management, problem tenants, natural disasters, insurance headaches, and fluctuating interest rates can all make an investor wish she had stuffed her money under the mattress instead of putting it into property. REIT stocks are subject to the fads and shifting investor sentiment in the broad stock market. Despite the risks, investors are attracted to real estate because it offers substantial current income and long-term appreciation as properties increase in value over time. It has a low correlation with stocks and bonds, which can help diversify your portfolio. In addition, since commercial leases almost always contain clauses that provide for rent increases, REITs are fairly inflation proof. So the answer to the question of whether REITs are good investments is—it depends. Your investment goals, tolerance for risk, time frame and personality are all factors.

If you want to know more, a good place to start is the National Association of REITs (NAREIT) web site: www.investinginreits.com. There you will find some excellent articles and a list of all publicly-traded REITs, along with links to many of them. Other places to further your education are www.reitnet.com, www.morningstar.com and www.reitcafe.com.

Buying Hens at the Real Estate Market

THE BOTTOM LINE

- REITs are moderate growth, high dividend investments that must pay out at least ninety percent of their annual taxable incomes to shareholders in the form of dividends.
- REITs fall into one of these three major categories: publicly traded, non-exchange traded and private.
- The two primary types of REITs are equity and mortgage.
- Publicly-traded equity REITs make up over ninety percent of the market.
- REITs provide a way for individual investors to invest in a basket of commercial properties along with a real estate business.
- REITs add diversity to your portfolio because of their low correlation with stocks and bonds.
- Investors make money with REITs through dividend payments and share price appreciation over time.
- The management team of a REIT may be the single most important factor in its success or failure.
- The measure of a REIT's performance is expressed as FFO or *funds from operations* to adjust for depreciation.
- REITs may be purchased from brokers, in mutual funds or directly from the company.
- REITs offer good protection from inflation.

Real estate cannot be lost or stolen, nor can it be carried away. Purchased with common sense, paid for in full, and managed with reasonable care, it is about the safest investment in the world.
—FRANKLIN D. ROOSEVELT

INVESTMENTS AND RETIREMENT PLANNING

"Yes, some mutual fund managers have used bad judgment from time to time. One ordered red wine with fish, another wore white after Labor day. Of course, the media blew it all out of proportion."

CHAPTER SEVEN

The Mega Market of Mutual Funds

THE FIRST MUTUAL FUND in the United States made its debut in 1924 when three Boston executives pooled their capital to form the Massachusetts Investors Trust. This fund, which is still operating today, remained somewhat of an anomaly for awhile, but the number of mutual funds on the market has exploded in the last few decades. A 2005 article in the *New York Times* quotes a statistic from the Investment Company Institute which states that more than half of American households invest in mutual funds. If you have a retirement plan, it is very likely you own at least one of them. But exactly what are they and how do you choose from the mind-boggling array of offerings you can find in this marketplace? That is what this chapter is all about.

What Is a Mutual Fund?

A *mutual fund* is a basket of securities owned by a pool of investor capital. Each investor buys shares of the entire basket, which may contain stocks, bonds, cash instruments, or some combination of these. By bringing together a group of people with small amounts to invest, mutual funds enable everyone to buy a larger piece of the market than anyone could buy on her own. The concept sounds good, but don't get lulled into a false sense of security—not all mutual funds are created equal. They vary according to management style, objectives, asset mix, size, and risk levels.

Learning Your Way Around the Market

There are now more mutual funds on the market than individual stocks. So many funds—how do you choose? We will begin by separating them into more manageable chunks, starting with asset classes.

Money Market Mutual Funds

Money market mutual funds invest in short-term debt instruments such as T-bills, commercial paper, bankers' acceptances, and certificates of deposit (CDs). They may be taxable or tax-free funds. Although CDs may offer a slightly higher return, money market mutual funds offer the benefit of liquidity with no penalty for withdrawals. Many allow you to write a limited number of checks from your account so you have immediate access to your cash. They are a safe place for your emergency funds and a good interest-bearing parking spot for cash while you are deciding what to do next. The downside of money market mutual funds is their low return compared to other types of investments.

Bond Funds

Bonds serve two primary purposes in your portfolio: one is to provide income on a steady basis, and the other is to add diversity. Since funds hold quantities of bonds that do not mature at the same time, they are described by their approximate maturity. If most holdings are for less than three years, the fund is called a short-term or limited bond fund. Intermediate funds hold bonds that mature in three to ten years, and long-term funds hold bonds with maturities of ten years or more. As with individual bonds, the longer the term, the higher the yield because of the increased interest rate risk. There are bond funds for every type of bond in existence, including:

- U.S. Government bond funds. Composed largely of Treasury bonds, these are considered the safest of the bond funds.

- Mortgage-backed securities funds hold bonds issued by government agencies (such as Fannie Mae).
- Corporate bond funds. These funds are made up of bonds issued by corporations. They have a higher risk of default because they are only as good as the creditworthiness of the companies that issue them. This increased risk translates to higher returns than government bonds.
- Municipal bond funds. State and local governments issue bonds when they need to raise funds for public projects such as parks and schools. Munis are popular with high-income investors because most municipal bonds are exempt from federal taxes, and often from state taxes as well. The tax-free feature usually does not benefit those in lower tax brackets.
- Foreign bond funds invest in bonds issued by foreign governments and corporations.
- Global bond funds invest in bonds all over the world, including the United States.
- High-yield bond funds. Who wouldn't want the highest yield? Perhaps well-informed people like you who know high-yield bonds are also known as junk bonds. These funds hold the bonds of companies with low credit ratings or no credit at all. Remember: high yield equals high risk.
- Multi-sector or balanced bond funds. These funds may hold a mixed bag of some combination of the different types listed above, as well as any other type of bond that exists. For example, a multi-sector fund may hold government, corporate, international, and high-yield bonds. Their main goal is to provide current income with a moderate level of risk.

Investors may choose bond funds over purchasing individual bonds because they want professional management or more diversification. Bond mutual funds pay interest monthly, and this is automatically reinvested unless the investor chooses to receive income payments. Another plus is the liquidity offered by a fund, especially the ones that allow you to write checks on the account. On the flip side, a bond fund's lack of fixed maturity date means there is no specific time when you are guaranteed to get all your money back. Payment amounts from the bond fund can vary according to its holdings. In addition, just as with equity funds, you will have to pay your portion of the fund's capital gains tax even if you did not buy into the fund until just before it paid dividends. (We will discuss this in more detail later in this chapter). Your risk level can vary dramatically depending on the type of bond fund selected. Funds that invest primarily in government and corporate debt are fairly low risk, but a fund holding high-yield (junk bonds) is not for the faint-of-heart.

Stock Funds

This is largest category of mutual funds, and there are as many different types of funds as there are types of stocks. You can find funds classified by size, objective, location, sector, or a combination of these. You can even find specialty funds such as those with selections chosen for their ethical considerations or their environmental records. Here are some examples:

By Size or Market Cap:
- Large-cap funds. Investors who choose these are often looking for income from dividends paid.
- Mid-cap funds and small-cap funds invest in mid-size and small companies that have the potential for returns through growth.

By Objective:
- Income funds are for investors seeking current dividends for income. These funds are popular with retirees and are generally composed of blue chip companies.
- Growth funds. These funds contain stocks the managers believe have the greatest earnings growth potential. Emphasis may be placed on small-cap stocks, but the funds are not limited to these.
- Value funds. Composed of stocks the managers believe are undervalued. These can be any cap size.
- Blend funds. A combination of growth and value stocks.

By Location:
- International or Foreign Funds. These funds invest only in stocks and bonds outside the United States.
- Global Funds. Global funds may choose investments from any country in the world, including the United States.

- Regional Funds. The focus is on a single area of the world, such as Asia or Latin America.
- Country Funds. Funds from specific countries, such as China.

By Specialty:
- Sector Funds. This type of fund concentrates on stocks selected from a single segment of the economy, such as energy, utility or technical stocks. REIT funds are in this category.
- Socially-Responsible Funds. Also called Ethical Funds, holdings are screened using certain guidelines. For example, some funds may not invest in industries such as tobacco, firearms, or alcohol; others shun companies believed to exploit labor or that have poor environmental records.

You can see there is a lot of room for overlap—another reason why it is important to read the prospectus. If you are not diligent in your research, you can end up with several funds that appear to have different strategies, but that all hold the same stocks.

> Don't gamble. Take all your savings and buy some good stock and hold it till it goes up, then sell it. If it don't go up, don't buy it.
> —Will Rogers

Hybrid Funds

Hybrid, or asset allocation funds, are a combination of stocks and bonds in a single basket, and some of them include money market instruments as well. These funds are usually categorized either by their level of risk or by their objective. They may be actively or passively managed (more about this later) and the variety on the market is limited only by the imagination of the mutual fund managers. You will even find funds of funds that are baskets of—you guessed it—other mutual funds. Here are some types you will see advertised:

- Balanced Funds invest in a combination of fixed-income securities (bonds and sometimes cash instruments) and equities (stocks) in order to achieve a stated objective. Balanced growth funds will hold more stocks while balanced conservative funds will hold more fixed income securities. You will find a fund's percentage of each asset class in its prospectus.
- Life Cycle Funds are also known as Age-Based Funds. The allocation between equities and fixed income investments is adjusted as the years pass, becoming more conservative and income-oriented as the investor ages.

- Lifestyle Funds take not only the investor's age into consideration in determining the asset allocation, but also her tolerance for risk and desired objective. They can be conservative, moderate, or aggressive.
- Target Date Funds are like life cycle funds, except these are designed to reach their stated objectives by a specific date in the future, which is most often the planned retirement day. Adjustments are made to the mix of assets in the fund, becoming more conservative as the target date nears. This is referred to as a "glide path" in the mutual fund world.

To Manage or Not To Manage— That Is the Question

All mutual funds are managed one of two ways—actively or passively. The ads you see and hear constantly are usually for actively-managed funds. These have a fund manager, a professional who selects what goes in the basket within the guidelines of the prospectus. When investors feel uncertain about handling their own portfolios, buying into an actively-managed fund is a relatively inexpensive way to "hire" a portfolio manager. One of the most important considerations with this type of fund is to find out all you can about the individual(s) in charge. How successful has she been in making money for her shareholders? It is vital to understand her preferred method for evaluating stocks to make sure it agrees with your philosophy. Is she high-risk and speculative? Low-risk and conservative? Does she look for undervalued stocks? Growth stocks? Large companies? Small ones? Does she stay on target according to the objectives for the fund or does she tend to drift among investing styles? How long has she been in charge of the fund? This will tell you if the fund's return history is the result of her work or of a previous manager's. It is important for you to know that the manager's salary is based on the amount of assets contained in the fund—which means she makes money even if you do not.

Look carefully at an actively-managed fund's expenses, because high fees can erode any gains you make. You will find this information in the mutual fund prospectus (the legal document that contains the rules and regulations for the particular fund), as well as its objec-

The Mega Market of Mutual Funds

tives. You would probably rather have a root canal than read it, but trust me, it's worth the effort. Before long, you will learn to cut through the jargon and zero in on the information you need.

If you do not want to choose your own stocks or trust a mutual fund manager to do it for you, the simplest, cheapest option is to invest in a passively-managed *index fund*. When you hear financial reporters describe the stock market by saying, "The Dow is up so many points today, and the NASDAQ is down," they are actually talking about *indexes*. Indexes are statistical measures the economists have developed because it would be impossible to track the performance of every single stock. Just as television raters or political pollsters survey representative samples of our population to come to conclusions about national trends, indexes are a selected portfolio of stocks used as a sample to track market trends. Index funds are designed to simply follow these trends.

> Education is what you get when you read the fine print. Experience is what you get when you don't.
> —PETE SEEGER

Index Funds

Following the "if you can't beat them, join them" philosophy, John Bogle, founder and former chair of the Vanguard Group, conceived the first index fund. This passive investing does not attempt to beat the market—just match it. The idea is based on a theory called *Efficient Market Hypothesis* that says, in a nutshell, it is impossible to beat the market consistently without unacceptably high risks. An index fund, then, is a mutual fund that attempts to mirror a particular index.

We know large-cap stocks are different animals from small caps so, as you might expect, they have their own indexes. Here are the most well known indexes:

- The **Dow Jones Industrial Average** tracks the thirty largest companies in the United States—the blue chips. The Dow has been around since 1896 and is the one most frequently referred to as "the market." The Dow is owned by Dow Jones & Company, the people that publish *The Wall Street Journal*.
- The **Standard & Poor's 500 Index** also tracks large-cap stocks, and includes 500 of them in its portfolio. The S&P 500 covers all major areas of the U.S. economy . A selection committee

reviews the holdings several times each year and may make as many as fifty changes depending on performance. The S&P 500 is considered the benchmark for large-cap stocks, and this is the index most actively-managed fund managers strive to beat.
- The **NASDAQ Composite Index** (the NASDAQ) represents the more than 4,000 stocks that trade on the NASDAQ exchange. It is heavily weighted with technology, internet and small-cap stocks, making it more volatile than the first two.
- The **Wilshire 5000 Total Market Index**. Despite its name, the number of stocks in this index varies. Presently, it tracks about 5,100, but in the past it has monitored more than 6,500 stocks. It covers virtually all of the public companies headquartered in the United States, and is the most diversified index in the world.
- The **Russell 2000 Index** tracks the performance of 2,000 small-cap stocks from various industries. There are a number of Russell Indexes, but this one is the most widely used index for small caps.

There are many, many more indexes that track nearly any market you can think of. The important thing to remember about indexes is they are great tools to tell us the direction and trend of the market, and to use as benchmarks to measure the performance of an investment portfolio. Suppose, for example, your portfolio of small-cap stocks earned ten percent this year. Sound good? Maybe—until you find out the Russell 2000 increased by fifteen percent during the same time period. You can't judge performance without something to compare it to.

The difference between the performance of an index fund and its benchmark is referred to as its *tracking error*. Since perfect tracking would be nearly impossible to achieve, a tracking error of about 0.25 percent is generally accepted. There is no need for the fund manager to pick stocks—it can all be done by computer—so this can mean much lower fees.

Exchange-Traded Funds

With names like "Spiders" and "Vipers," you may think you have wandered into a jungle, but you have actually arrived at the newest section of the marketplace. *Exchange-traded funds* came on the scene in 1993, and the popularity of this hybrid offering is growing. Exchange-traded funds are baskets of securities, but they are not mutual funds. They are passively-managed and most of them track an index, but they are not index funds, either. So what are they? Exchange-traded funds are baskets of securities that (usually) track an index but trade like individual stocks. You buy and sell them on a stock exchange, which means their prices change throughout the trading day. These baskets can hold not only stocks and bonds, but commodities and precious metals as well.

Exchange-traded funds, like any other investment, have their pros and cons. On the pro side, you can buy and sell them easily, and their expense ratios are about as low as you can find anywhere. There are no minimum investment requirements, so you can buy as little as one share if you want to, and that leads to their biggest drawback, which are the brokerage fees incurred from buying and selling them. They also have not proved to be as proficient in tracking as regular index funds. Your personality and investment objectives will determine if you should consider these products. There are some good references in the last chapter to help you learn more, and the guidance of a trusted financial professional can be invaluable.

How Investors Make Money with Mutual Funds

Okay. You now know something about the different types of funds. Let's talk about how they can help you reach your investment goals. There are three ways you can earn returns by investing in mutual funds:

1. Dividends and interest. Most funds give you the option of reinvesting the earnings to buy more shares in the fund, which is an excellent way to build your net worth. If you need the income, you may request that the fund send you periodic checks.
2. Capital gains. When the fund sells stocks that have increased

in value, it earns profits (capital gains), which it divides proportionately among shareholders. Record keeping is easy because the fund's overseers keep track of everything for you. At the end of each year, the mutual fund sends an IRS Form 1099 to each of its investors that summarizes the fund's cash distributions and tax liability. To be taxed as capital gains, stocks must be held at least one year and a day. If held less than that, you will pay tax on gains at your ordinary income tax rate. In a taxable account, this could be significant.

3. Share price appreciation. Stocks held in the fund that increase in value drive prices for mutual fund shares higher, which means you can sell your fund shares for a profit. You can sell your shares quickly and easily at any time, giving you the benefit of liquidity.*

> A clever arrangement of bad eggs will never make a good omelette.
> —C. S. Lewis

Just like every other investment type, it is important to think through your reasons for buying a fund. What is your objective? How much risk are you willing to take? What is your personal style? How will a fund help you diversify your henhouse? How successful you are in making gains depends on how wisely you choose your fund, so let's look at that next.

Shopping Strategies

Pricing a mutual fund is pretty straightforward: the total of a fund's assets minus its liabilities equals its *net asset value* or NAV. To calculate the price per share of the mutual fund, divide the total NAV by the total number of shares in the fund. The NAV changes continuously as people buy and sell shares and the value of the fund's holdings fluctuate, but the official price is quoted only once at the end of each trading day. Comparing prices is not a very effective way of selecting a fund to buy, so how do you choose one? We're back to that prospectus again. It is truly the only way for you to find the informa-

---

* For any trade, SEC regulations say that you have three days before the money is available to you. When you buy something, you have three days to pay for it.

The Mega Market of Mutual Funds

tion you need to make an informed decision. Here are some things to look for among the verbiage:

Objective

Make sure you understand what the fund invests in and why. *All* fund managers say they want to increase the bottom line—what you want to know is *how* they plan to do it. Also, consider the fund's risk level to see if the volatility is within your tolerance level.

Style

If it is an actively-managed fund, how consistent has the manager been in staying within the stated objectives of the fund? Has she stayed on course? Or has she demonstrated a tendency to drift into following the latest trends?

Performance

Avoid jumping on the bandwagon of the latest high-flyer. Remember, a rising tide lifts all boats, and a good recent performance is not necessarily because of a manager's superior stock picking. At the same time, do not put too much stock in past performance, either. Instead, look at the long-term returns of the fund to see if they have been consistent. An index fund is easier to evaluate. If it does not mirror the index it tracks pretty closely, pass it up because something is wrong.

A Load of What?

The biggest drawback of mutual funds is the costs associated with them. Fees, many of them hidden under layers of jargon, are often the main reason funds end up with less than stellar performances. Here are the terms to look for:

> The large print giveth, and the small print taketh away.
> —TOM WAITS

Loads. Quite simply, this is a commission paid to the broker or salesperson from whom you buy the fund. There are different types, depending on the type of shares you buy. The most common types are A, B, and C shares. "A" shares have a front-end load, which means the commissions are collected up front when you buy the fund. If you buy "B" shares, you pay back-end loads, aka deferred sales charges. This means you are paying the commission on an installment plan. If you sell the fund before a designated date, you will pay a penalty. The longer you hold the fund, the less you pay. "C" shares have no load, but they have higher expenses. C shares are the broker's answer to *no-load funds*. "A" shares are usually the best deal because expenses are lower and there is no penalty for getting out of the fund.

Some experts advocate buying only no-load funds, but it can be a mistake to use this as your sole criteria for decision-making. If a load and a no-load fund hold the same stocks, a no-load will probably perform better, but sometimes no-load funds can have other fees that will offset your savings. Make sure you are comparing apples to apples when shopping for a fund.

Management Expense Ratio (MER) gives you information about ongoing annual fees. It includes:

- The cost of hiring the fund manager, aka the management fee, typically between 0.5% and 1% of the assets. This may sound like a small amount—until you multiply it by the millions of dollars held in a fund. It is clear why mutual fund managers are among the top earners in this country, even though many of them fail to outperform the market averages.
- Administrative costs such as postage, supplies or record-keeping. Some funds are very frugal while others are more extravagant in their spending.
- *12B-1 Fees*. These fees are used to pay distribution expenses, such as the cost of printing and mailing prospectuses, and advertising costs. You know all those ads you see for mutual funds? Now you know who is footing the bill for them.

Study after study shows no correlation between high expense ratios and high returns. This is one time when "you get what you pay for" ain't necessarily so.

> In my opinion, buying a load fund is the equivalent of stepping up to bat with two strikes already against you. Your investment first has to earn enough money to cover the load, or commission cost, before it can start to work for you.
> —BURTON MALKIEL

Other Considerations: Timing, Turnover, and the Price of Fame

Perhaps as important as *what* you buy is *when* you buy it. Most experts advise against purchasing a mutual fund at the end of the year in a taxable account, because that is when the fund usually makes distributions. By law, a mutual fund must pay out at least ninety percent of its capital gains and dividends each year, and this usually happens in December. Distributions trigger capital gains taxes, regardless of whether or not you reinvest them. A capital gain is just a fancy accounting term for profit—the difference between the buying price and the selling price of an asset and, as previously mentioned, has to do with the length of time an asset is held in your portfolio. In a mutual fund, responsibility for this tax is divided among shareholders, including those who just joined the party. If you buy into a mutual fund in a taxable account right before it pays dividends, you will be hit with capital gains tax on profits made before you even got there.

The *turnover rate* indicates the amount of buying and selling that has transpired during the year. More trades equals more trading costs, so mutual funds that have a high turnover rate can cost you plenty. Actively-managed funds with managers attempting to beat an index will have far more trades than passively-managed funds.

Too much success can be bad for a fund. Investors all want to place their money on a winner, so cash pours into a fund that is doing well until, eventually, it gets so big the fund manager has a hard time finding enough good investments to buy and the overall return suffers. The official term for this problem is "dilution."

Consulting the Stars

Morningstar is a popular resource for stock and mutual fund investors. This well-respected company offers independent investment research and analysis along with abundant articles and learning tools on its website at www.morningstar.com. Morningstar statisticians compare similar funds and rank them based on how well they have performed in relationship to one another. They assign each fund a rating of from one to five stars based entirely on their mathematical calculations of past performance. Here is what the stars mean:

- Five stars are given to the top ten percent of funds in the group
- Four stars are given to the next twenty-two percent
- Three stars are given to the middle thirty-five percent
- Two stars are given to the next twenty-two percent
- One star is given to the bottom ten percent of funds in the group

Morningstar has popularized a tool they call a "style box," which is a graphic illustration of a fund's characteristics. It looks like a flat view of a Rubik's cube, but fortunately is much less complicated than that. The vertical axis relates to size—large, medium, and small; the horizontal axis relates to style—value, growth or a blend of the two. This makes a total of nine squares, (three rows up, and three rows across) that are used to classify an equity mutual fund into one of these categories:

Fig. 4: Morningstar Style Box™

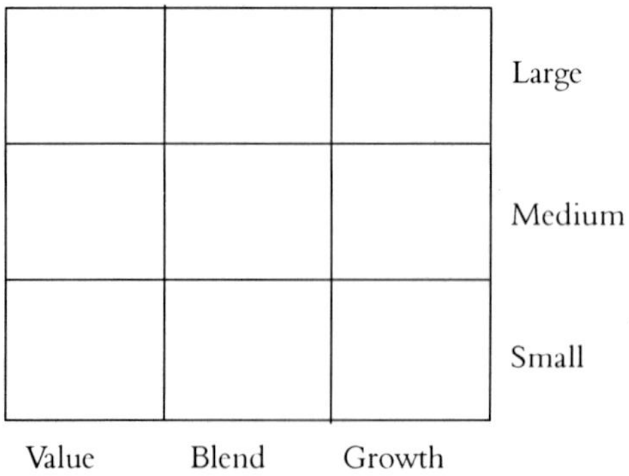

- Large value
- Large blend
- Large growth
- Medium value
- Medium blend
- Medium growth
- Small value
- Small blend
- Small growth

You can use this tool to make sure you are comparing apples to apples. The style box is useful for categorizing funds and you can use it as an asset allocation tool with your stocks. There are certainly many other research sites, but I singled this one out because it is so well known and widely used. Morningstar's website is chock-full of free services, but you can get much more in-depth analysis with a premium (paid) membership. If the price tag puts you off, many public libraries have subscriptions to the service. I should mention that Morningstar does not cover the entire universe of mutual funds—funds must have at least three years of history to receive a rating.

The Mega Market of Mutual Funds

Putting It All Together

One day Ima Investor takes a walk through her henhouse and finds she has an empty roost in her stock section. Because she needs a whole flock of hens, she decides the best way to fill it is by buying a mutual fund. Her first step is to sort through the thousands of funds available to find the top few that meet her requirements. Ima has twenty-five years until she plans to retire and knows she can afford to take a little more risk, so she decides to focus on small-cap funds. She is a dedicated bargain hunter, so she leans toward the value style of investing. With these criteria in mind, Ima has a number of ways to search for funds. She can consult with her financial advisor, she can browse websites that offer fund research, and she can browse through hundreds of articles about mutual funds in the financial press. Ima decides she will screen for funds on the web, then ask for her advisor's opinion of her selections.

Using a fund screener on the internet, Ima fills in the blanks with the requested information. It asks her for the fund type she is seeking (small value), the minimum amount she has to invest, whether she wants a load fund (she does not), and the risk level she is willing to accept. It also asks her to choose the number of years of fund performance she wants to see (she chooses the longest period offered), and the minimum return (percentage) she is looking for. Her entries produce the names of several funds with NAVs in her price range, so she chooses the two with the most stars to study further. Ima's candidates each received four stars from Morningstar. This is excellent information but not enough for her to make a decision. She must dig deeper.

Her next step is to closely examine each fund she is considering. The first thing she does is to check out each fund's top holdings so she can get an idea of the types of stocks the manager likes to buy. She peruses each manager's biography to determine her experience level and tenure with the fund, her philosophy, and anything else she can read between the lines. Ima will make no decision until she has examined the prospectuses. She can request a printed copy from the fund, but many now have their prospectuses online.

While Ima is doing her research, her friend and fellow egg farmer, Shara Broadmarket, stops by to chat. Shara tells Ima she has filled her entire henhouse using index funds, and suggests Ima com-

> I tell people [investing] should be dull. It shouldn't be exciting. Investing should be more like watching paint dry or watching grass grow. If you want excitement, take $800 and go to Las Vegas.
> —Paul Samuelson

pare her two candidates to a small-cap value index fund. Ima takes Shara's advice and finds the difference between the expenses of the index fund and the actively-managed funds is only one percent annually. This sounds like an insignificant amount but just to be sure, Ima calls her financial advisor to get her opinion. Her advisor tells her the small percentage can make a huge difference in the long run and that most studies conclude it is very difficult (although it has been done) for fund managers to beat the returns of low-cost index funds. Ima decides she has enough to worry about already, so she buys the index fund.

Are index funds better? The answer is—it depends. (You knew that was coming, didn't you?) They often outperform actively-managed mutual funds, but on the down side, index funds do not give you the potential for big gains over market return. It all comes back to what kind of investor you are. If you enjoy the thrill of a roller coaster, index funds may seem boring, but if you like a nice, steady ride and want consistent returns, they may be just the ticket.

Buying Funds

You can purchase mutual funds through brokers, banks, or financial planners, and you can buy some funds by contacting the fund companies directly. Fund supermarkets are popular one-stop shops where you can buy funds of many different companies. Large brokerages such as Vanguard, Fidelity and others offer this service.

If you decide to research funds, there is no shortage of data out there—in fact, sometimes the volume is overwhelming. To help you cut through the chatter, here are some of the best sources for information about mutual funds on the web in addition to Morningstar. The Mutual Fund Education Alliance is a non-profit trade association of the no-load mutual fund industry. Their website is www.mfea.com/FundSelector. The Wall Street Journal's site at www.wallstreetjournal.com has a great mutual fund screener. You can research any funds that look interesting and even download a prospectus for most of them. Virtually every online brokerage has re-

The Mega Market of Mutual Funds

search tools, or check out www.smartmoney.com for still more. That should be enough to keep you busy for awhile.

> Investing is a marathon, not a sprint. Once you reach retirement, you'll care little whether you won the race in any given year. But you will take satisfaction in crossing the finish line by achieving financial security for your golden years.
> —JOHN BRENNAN

The Bottom Line

- Mutual funds are popular because they are convenient, simple to buy and offer great diversity and liquidity. Today, there are more mutual funds than stocks on the market.
- Mutual funds vary according to management style, objectives, asset mix, size, and risk levels.
- Hybrid, or asset allocation funds, are a combination of stocks and bonds in a single basket, and some of them include money market instruments as well.
- All mutual funds are managed one of two ways—actively or passively. Actively-managed funds have higher fees than passively-managed funds.
- Fees can seriously erode your bottom line.
- An index fund is a mutual fund that attempts to mirror a particular index.
- Exchange-traded funds are baskets of securities that usually track an index, but trade like stocks.
- The three ways you can earn returns by investing in mutual funds are dividends and interest, capital gains and share price appreciation.
- The official price, or NAV, of a mutual fund is quoted only once at the end of each trading day.
- A load is a commission paid to a salesperson for selling the fund to you.
- The most important things to do when considering a mutual fund is to read the prospectus and to do your homework.

CHAPTER EIGHT

Browsing at the Specialty Market

I REMEMBER HOW EXCITING it was the first time I went into a casino in Las Vegas. With dollar signs in my eyes and high hopes in my heart, I plunked some coins into a slot machine and stood there expectantly waiting for something to happen. Then I realized something had happened—I'd lost my money. Gambling was not as much fun as I thought it would be. But there are people who find mutual funds dull and bonds boring enough to induce a coma. They love to take risks and play for high stakes, and this is the marketplace where they shop.

> The safest way to double your money is to fold it over once and put it in your pocket.
>
> —Kin Hubbard

Hedge Funds

Like a mutual fund, a *hedge fund* pools your investment capital with that of others, but that is where the similarities end. A mutual fund manager has a dual focus. She wants to beat a benchmark, usually an index, and to do better than competing fund managers, but this does not necessarily imply a positive number. For example, if the benchmark for the fund is down ten percent and the mutual fund is only down eight percent, the manager has beaten the index. You have still lost your money, just not as much as if it had been in another investment—take comfort where you can find it. The focus of a hedge fund manager is to earn a positive return—always.

INVESTING STARTING FROM SCRATCH

When it comes to management, you can think of a hedge fund as the polar opposite of a passively-managed index fund. Hedge funds are smaller, actively-managed, and nimble—they may dart in and out of investments. The manager usually has a great deal of her own money at stake in the fund and is considered a superstar investor. This is what attracts people; investing in a hedge fund is a partnership with a high-rolling manager.

Mutual fund managers are generally compensated based on the amount of assets in the fund—the larger the fund grows, the more money they earn. A hedge fund manager's compensation is asset-based *and* performance-based. This means the more money she makes for you, the more she makes for herself in both returns and fees. That is quite a performance incentive.

One of the main differences between mutual fund managers and hedge fund managers is not *what* they invest in, but *how* they go about it. Because hedge funds are not regulated by the SEC, managers are free to use higher risk strategies such as leverage, selling short and hedging with derivatives (we will get to these in the next section). They may also hold most of their eggs in one basket by taking concentrated positions in just one investment, or even buy illiquid investments you would not find in a mutual fund. Instead of a prospectus, a hedge fund manager uses an *offering memorandum* to outline her investment objectives.

In a mutual fund, you can choose to take distributions of earnings if you want them. Most hedge funds are limited partnerships. Earnings are not distributed to the partners (investors), but are retained in the fund. As we have already discussed, whether you take them or leave them, you must pay capital gains taxes on earnings. Hedge funds are not liquid; you cannot just sell shares when you want your money out. There is a prescribed length of time your money must remain in the fund.

Hedge funds tend to be smaller than mutual funds with most holding less than $250 million in assets. They are also selective and geared toward high net worth investors. These may be individuals or entities such as pension funds, endowments, or foundations. Lest you put all your eggs in one manager's basket, most hedge fund investors achieve diversity by holding a number of hedge funds that employ different strategies. There are even funds of hedge funds

> Hedge funds are for wealthy investors willing to take risks.

110

Browsing at the Specialty Market

for those who don't want to construct their own portfolios, with a manager of managers who typically charges a fee on top of the fees charged by the funds themselves. It is not difficult to see why they must achieve large, positive returns.

"Yes, we have *Chicken Soup For The Investor's Soul*. Do you want to pay cash or buy it on margin?"

Buying on Margin

Buying on margin is a high-risk strategy that can yield jackpot profits—or cost you everything you have (and then some). This technique uses leverage—or borrowed money—to allow you to purchase securities without actually shelling out the cash. In order to use this technique, you must first establish a margin account with your broker. The initial deposit to open the account is called the minimum margin. The amount will vary depending on the brokerage, but you can count on depositing at least $2,000. After the account has been opened, you will be able to borrow money to buy securities. Most brokers will lend up to fifty percent of the value of the security, but the percentage varies depending upon what it is you want to buy. Not all stocks can be bought on margin. The Federal Reserve Board has regulations in place about which stocks are eligible and which are not, and your brokerage may have further restrictions.

> Who goeth a borrowing
> Goeth a sorrowing.
> —Thomas Tusser

Here is how it works: Let's say you found a stock you want to buy but you don't want to tie up all your money to make the purchase, so you deposit the required amount into your margin account. The percentage of these funds that you use to buy your stock is called the initial margin. The maintenance margin is the minimum balance you must retain in your account at all times. If the value of the stock decreases below the maintenance margin, you will get a margin call from your broker asking you to either sell your stock or deposit more money. If you fail to do this, the brokerage has the right to sell stock in order to make up the shortage—they have their bets covered.

I will clarify all this with an example. Because of her experience as a chicken wrangler, Ima Investor has a powerful hunch Acme Chicken Wire stock is about to skyrocket. The stock is priced at $100 per share and she wants to buy 200 shares. That will cost her $20,000, but she only has $10,000 she wants to invest. She decides to go for broke (literally), so she deposits her $10,000 into her margin account. Then she borrows the other $10,000 from her broker and buys the stock. Now she owns 200 shares of Acme stock and has a debt of $10,000. This is twice what she could have bought without using leverage. It turns out Ima was right—Acme stock increases twenty-five percent to $125 a share. She decides to quit while she is ahead, so she sells the stock. Her profits look like this:

Browsing at the Specialty Market

Sale of stock:	$25,000 (200 shares @ $125 per share)
Repayment of margin loan:	−$10,000
Original investment:	−$10,000
Ima's gain:	$ 5,000

Without using leverage, Ima would have only been able to buy 100 shares, earning $2,500. That would translate into a twenty-five percent return on her investment, which is pretty darn good, but by using leverage, Ima hit the jackpot and made a fifty percent return ($5,000 on a $10,000 investment).

What if Ima had been wrong about Acme's prospects? What if instead of going up twenty-five percent, it had taken a nosedive and lost twenty-five percent of its value? The picture would not be near as pretty. It would look like this:

Sale of stock:	$15,000 (200 shares @ $75 per share)
Repayment of margin loan:	−$10,000
Original investment:	−$10,000
Ima's loss:	−$ 5,000

Ima lost twice what she would have if she had not bought on margin. In fact, if she had not bought the stock on margin, she might not have lost anything. She might have decided to hold onto it for the long haul hoping it would rally and the price would eventually reward her confidence. These examples don't take other costs into consideration, like commissions and interest.

Like all loans, as soon as it is made the interest meter starts ticking, so buying on margin is mainly used for investments only meant to be held for a short time. Do you even want to think about what would have happened to poor Ima if the stock had lost fifty percent of its value? She would have lost more than 100% of her investment. Yowzer!

> You can never predict when that unknown torpedo will come out of the dark and smash the price of a stock.
>
> —RALPH SEGER

Short Selling

Often you will hear investors described as taking "long" or "short" positions. In a nutshell, long positions make money when the price of an asset goes up, and short positions make money when the price of an asset goes down. Sometimes you hear long positions described as "bullish" and short positions described as "bearish." Investors who engage in selling short are confident prices will fall—so confident that they sell stock they don't even own in order to reap the profit. How is that possible? Like this: first, you must have a margin account with sufficient funds to be used as collateral for a loan. Next, you borrow the desired stock from the broker. The broker may have the stock you want in her own account or she may get it from someone else's account who has agreed to lend. Then you sell the shares. The proceeds from the sale are deposited into a brokerage account, which earns interest. Unfortunately, you don't get to keep all that interest—part of it goes to the broker and part of it goes to the lender of the shares. When the anticipated drop in the price of the stock occurs, you "cover the short" by buying shares on the open market and returning them to the broker. Then you pocket the difference between the original selling price and the new, lower price and everyone is happy.

So what can go wrong? Plenty. If the stock you borrowed pays dividends, you must continue to pay those to the lender. And if the stock should split while it is shorted, you will owe twice as many shares as you borrowed. There is also the excellent possibility you have guessed wrong and the stock price goes up instead of down. If a lot of short sellers see the price of a stock beginning to rise and they all start covering their shorts (buying) at the same time, the price will be driven even higher. Even if you guessed right and the stock price does fall, the key question is *when*? Can you hold on long enough to pay the interest and margin calls? As the English economist Lord John Keynes once noted, "Markets can stay irrational longer than you can stay solvent." When you buy a stock and it goes south, the most you can lose is one-hundred percent of your investment, but with short selling there is unlimited downside risk. If you don't cut your losses and cover the short, you can watch the price of a stock continue to go up and up. This unpleasant turn of events is called a "runaway short." You may get a margin call and be forced to sell in a rising market; this is known as a "short squeeze." You may also get a call at any time demanding the loan (of stock) be repaid. In that instance, you are left with the option of borrowing the stock from someone else or buying it on the open market.

Derivatives

A *derivative* is a type of investment that derives its value from another asset. It is a contract between two or more parties with a value based on the underlying assets. The assets can be anything—stocks, bonds, commodities, currencies, or market indexes—there are even contracts on the weather. The most common derivatives are *futures contracts*—commonly referred to just as *futures*—and *options*.

> Prediction is very difficult, especially if it's about the future.
> —NILS BOHR
> Nobel laureate in Physics

Commodities and Futures

Commodities are tangible, real items used to make the goods we use every day such as oil, grains, cotton, wool, soybeans, coffee, sugar and yes, pork bellies, just to name a few. These items are sold by farmers, miners, or producers to the manufacturers who make the end products we all buy. In the distant past, the sellers and buyers negotiated directly with each other, which as you can imagine, led to a great deal of anxiety about prices for both parties. Suppose you are a corn farmer and you have a bumper crop this year. Chances are your fellow corn farmers also have good yields because you all were subject to the same favorable conditions. You all show up at the marketplace to sell your crop at the same time because corn only lasts so long. With all that competition, there is a good chance you will be disappointed with the price your lovely ears fetch. If, on the other hand, you are a buyer for a cereal manufacturer, you are going to have a great time at this year's market haggling for low prices. Next year the shoes may be on the opposite feet. No one can predict the future—but that does not stop people from trying. In 1848, the first commodities exchange was founded in the U.S.—The Chicago Board of Trade (CBOT). The function of CBOT was, and still is, to create balance between supply and demand. It does this by developing standardized agreements between buyers and sellers called *futures contracts*, again generally referred to as just futures.

When you buy futures, you are agreeing to buy a fixed amount of an asset for a set price on a specific date in the future. The lengths of most contracts are from a few months up to two years. If the price of the asset goes up during the holding period, the buyer is happy, and if the price of the asset goes down, the seller is happy. With this kind of transaction, somebody always wins and somebody always loses. Protecting your interests in this way is an example of hedging, the technique used to reduce risk from unpredictable price moves. But we are not producers or manufacturers, we are investors—where do we fit into this picture? We enter the scene when we become *speculators*.

Investors who buy and sell futures are *speculators*, most often referred to as *traders*. They have no intention of ever taking delivery of a truckload of soybeans or pork bellies, but they do want to get in on the game of betting on the ultimate price of these goods. Every day, prices fluctuate because every day, things happen in the world that affect production of raw materials. There is a drought somewhere or a freeze hits. A hurricane or other natural disaster wreaks havoc. War breaks out or a government topples. The concept of trading futures is straightforward: decide whether you think prices of a certain commodity are going up (called "going long") or down (called "going short"), and hope you are right. The execution is far more complicated, but here is a nutshell version just to give you an idea of how it works.

In order to get in the game, you must prove you have the financial resources to withstand losses by opening an individual margin account, either with a futures broker, who must have a special commodities license, or directly with a futures commission merchant. The initial margin is a minimum deposit required for a trade, usually five to ten percent of the amount of the contract you want to buy. You could think of this as your ante to play. Variation margin or maintenance margin is paid as the hands are dealt. Prices of the underlying asset are monitored, and cash is moved between the accounts of those who have losses and those who have gains every single day during the period of the contract. If you lose more than the balance of the account, you must ante up and deposit more money. If you cannot pay, then the broker immediately closes out your position and you are out of the game.

Browsing at the Specialty Market

Since traders don't actually want to buy the commodity, they close out or liquidate their contracts well in advance of the expiration dates. This is referred to as "unwinding" the future position. Unlike other markets, the commodities market employs daily trading limits. There is a range set for each commodity that limits the amount of price fluctuation each day. When prices hit that limit, the exchange declares a "locked limit market," which means there will be times when you cannot sell your contract, no matter what.

If you would like some coaching, you can hire a commodity-trading advisor to give you expert advice and another opinion. Or, if you don't want to make trades yourself, you can open a managed account instead of an individual account and let someone else make the deals for you. You are still the one responsible for paying any losses, so choosing your stand-in, the account manager, is an extremely important decision. *Commodity pools* are similar to mutual funds in that funds are pooled to buy a group of commodities. Each pool is managed by a commodities broker, and profits and losses are calculated in proportion to the amount invested. The level of risk stays high, but at least you have company.

Today there are seven commodities exchanges in the United States. They still operate like you have seen in the movies—with floor traders shouting at each other and waving bits of paper in the air. This is aptly named the "open outcry system" and is the method by which prices are set. The Commodity Futures Trading Commission (CFTC) is the federal agency that oversees and regulates commodities trading. A futures contract establishes a fixed price for a commodity, but the price of the contract itself is never fixed. Commodities trading for hedgers—the people who really want to buy and sell stuff—is all about protecting against the uncertainties of supply and demand, but for traders, it is all about guessing which way the pendulum will swing. Traders have to keep up with world events, politics, and literally, which way the wind is blowing.

> Financial forecasting is like driving a car blindfolded with directions from a passenger who is looking out the back window.
> —WERNER DE BONDT

Tangible items are not the only things that have prices that go up and down. In the 1970s, financial futures came onto the scene and later, stock index futures. These are affected by interest rates, global events, currency fluctuations, and stock prices.

Options

Options are securities, just like stocks and bonds. Like other securities, they are bought and sold on an exchange. The largest exchange is the Chicago Board Options Exchange, which opened in 1973. You may hear it referred to as "see-bo" (CBOE). Options are also derivatives, like futures, but with an important difference. When you buy futures, you are obligated to buy or sell the underlying asset. When you buy options, you have the right to buy or sell the underlying asset, but not the obligation. In short, options are optional. Perhaps the easiest way to understand this is to relate it to something more familiar.

Suppose you are house hunting and find a property you really like. You talk to the owner and agree upon a price, but you are not quite ready to buy. You ask the owner if she will hold the property for you and she agrees, for a price. You give her a sum of money in exchange for her guarantee she will sell it to you later at the price you agreed upon today—you have bought an option. Of course, the owner is not going to wait forever, so she puts a time limit on the deal. By a certain date, you must either complete the transaction or forfeit your option payment. Before the time is up, you discover the house was designed by Frank Lloyd Wright and is worth twice what you negotiated, but the owner still has to sell it to you at the option price. You win. Or maybe upon further inspection you discover the house is riddled with termites and may collapse into a pile of dust at any time, so you decide not to buy. You win again—except for the loss of your option.

Now let's transfer that idea to the purchase of other assets. As we have already noted, there are many types of assets that can be optioned, but we will use stock for our discussion. Options can be bought or sold. Those who buy options are called "holders" and those who sell options are called "writers." Holders have the right, but not the obligation, to buy or sell the underlying asset, whereas writers may be called upon to complete the transactions they have offered. There are two types of options: calls and puts. There are buyers and sellers of calls and buyers and sellers of puts. We will look at each of them individually.

Call Options

A call option gives you the right to buy stock, for a specific price, known as the strike price, on or before a specific date. Buyers of calls want to lock in the price of a stock because they believe it is due to rise. They are bullish, but not to the point where they want to buy the stock. By buying a call option instead, they get to participate in any increases in the stock price without much downside. Their only risk is the price of the option. Call buyers are taking a short position.

Sellers of calls take a long position. They own the stock and do not want to sell it, but they are willing to take a risk in order to make some income while they are holding the stock for the long haul. They believe the price of their stock will remain steady for the short term of the option. If they are correct, and the price stays the same (or even decreases), the buyer will not exercise the option and the seller gets to pocket the option money, which is called the premium. If they are wrong, and the stock price does go up, they must sell it at the strike price. When the strike price of a call option is less than the current price in the open market, the option is said to be "in the money." If the opposite is true and the market price is more than the strike price, the option is said to be "out of the money."

Let's look at some examples of call options. Acme Chicken Wire is currently selling at $50 per share, but Ima Investor thinks it will rise to $60 or more soon. She buys a call option on the stock with a strike price of $55 and a maturity of three months. Sure enough, the next month the stock rises to $60. She is in the money, so Ima exercises her option and buys the stock for $55, making an instant gain of $5 per share. If she is wrong and the stock price heads south, Ima simply lets her out of the money option expire, and the seller pockets her premium. There is also the case Ima could be absolutely right about the prospects of the stock, but the rise in price does not happen for six months. Unless the anticipated move up happens in her allotted time frame, she loses—but at least she just loses her option money.

Now let's look at this transaction in reverse. Ima owns Acme stock and wants to hold it for the long haul, but she does not see much action on the price coming in the near future. She is pretty confident the price will remain below $60 per share. She wants to make a little money, so she sells a call option on her stock for $60 with a maturity of three months. If she is right and the price remains stable, the option is out of the money and expires worthless. The amount of the premium is pure profit to Ima. If she is wrong and the option is in the money, she will have to sell her shares for $60, even if they are selling for $70 (or more) on the market. She has put a ceiling on her profit.

Put Options

A put option gives you the right to sell a stock for a specific price on or before a designated date. Buying a put option is like buying an insurance policy that will protect you in the event of dramatic price drops for stock you own. Buyers of put options are concerned the price may fall—they are bearish. If the stock price goes up instead of down, then the value of the put option eventually becomes worthless, just like unused insurance.

The seller of a put option, on the other hand, is looking to buy stock at a favorable price. When you sell a put option, you agree to buy the underlying stock when it falls to a certain strike price. If the price does not fall, you get to keep the premium. The problem begins when the stock falls and then keeps falling—you are still obligated to buy at the strike price. When the strike price of a put option is more than the current market price, the option is in the money. If the strike price is less than the market price, the option is out of the money. For both calls and puts, when the price of a stock is equal to the strike price, the option is said to be at the money.

Let's look at some examples of put options. Ima Investor is holding Acme Chicken Wire for the long haul. It is currently trading at $55, but she is worried about a new competitor who has developed rustproof chicken wire with a lifetime guarantee. She fears her Acme stock may drop like a rock before too much longer if Acme cannot compete. She buys a three month put option with a strike price of $45. At least she can sleep at night knowing her stock cannot go below $45. She has put a floor under her stock and insured against major losses.

Now let's suppose Ima does not own Acme shares. She would like to, but thinks the current price of $55 is too high. If the stock fell to $45, she would buy it. So she sells a put option with a $45 strike price. If the price falls to the strike price (or below) before the put expires, Ima will pay $45 a share for the stock to the buyer of her put— even it is selling for less on the open market. Remember, writers (sellers) are obligated to finish what they have started.

When a holder sells her option or when a seller buys back an option she has written, they are said to be "closing their positions." Call options are worth more as the value of the underlying asset increases. Put options are just the opposite—they are worth more as the underlying asset decreases in value. Using options as a way to manage risk is called hedging. Using options as a way to take advantage of short-term fluctuations in price is called speculating. In reality, most options are never exercised. Most investors take their profits by trading their options. The CBOE states that only ten percent of options are exercised, sixty percent are sold, and thirty percent expire worthless.

We've talked about puts and calls. There are also straddles and strangles, verticals, butterflies and wingspreads and other types of options—but that is for another book.

All that Glitters

Gold and other precious metals like silver or platinum are alternative assets that are both tangible and liquid. Gold has been valued for eons—historians tell us it was used for money at least as far back as the fifth century B.C. You can buy into precious metal mutual funds or invest in gold futures, but some investors want to hold more than paper in their hands, they want the real thing. What kinds of investors want to buy physical gold? It appeals to cautious sorts who do not trust the markets, currency speculators, and those who want a hedge against inflation or disaster. It also appeals to people who wish to hide wealth. These people buy gold in bullion bars or as coins. Numismatic gold coins are collected and valued because they are rare. Bullion coins are common and valued only because they are gold.

> Bullion doesn't pay interest or dividends, nor does it grow or expand by itself. That's the price you pay for tranquility.
> —Pierre Lassonde

The price of gold is reset daily by the London Gold Pool, a group composed of five members of the London Bullion Market Association. Their price, known as the "Gold Fixing," is recognized as the benchmark for trading values. Twice a day, the five members chat by telephone and arrive at the spot price or current rate. It goes without saying (but I will anyway) that you should buy gold only from reputable dealers—all that glitters is not gold. Then there is that little problem of storage...

INVESTING STARTING FROM SCRATCH

Currency Trading

If you have ever traveled internationally, odds are the first thing you did upon arrival at your destination was to exchange money. You cannot pay a taxi driver in Tokyo, or purchase a gelato in Italy with U.S. dollars, so you must trade for yen or euros. Investing in currency trading is no different, except it happens on a much, much larger scale. The Foreign Exchange Market (*Forex*) is the over-the-counter market where all currencies of the world are traded. This is a virtual market where trading is done by computers in major financial centers around the world. When a market in one city is closing, another market in the next time zone is opening, so the action goes on twenty-four hours a day, five days each week. The dollar volume of trading is measured in the trillions, so it is by far the largest market in the world. "If it is so big," you may be asking yourself, "why haven't I heard much about it?" Because it has traditionally been the domain of world governments, investment banks and large international organizations dealing in huge numbers. These entities use the foreign exchange market as a hedge against currency fluctuations and as a way to buy and sell goods in the world market—just like your gelato—but on a grand scale. We have learned where there are hedgers, there are speculators. How do they fit into the picture? They didn't until 1971. They had their hands tied by something called the Bretton Woods Agreement, which prevented speculation in currency markets. Time for another short history lesson.

Prior to World War II, the gold standard was used by the nations of the world to fix exchange rates. Each government guaranteed that its currency was backed by a specific amount of gold, necessitating substantial reserves of the precious metal. When World War I began, huge military defense expenditures used up all of the reserves of the major European powers. They started printing money without the gold to back it up, so the gold standard was largely abandoned. Before the end of World War II, the Allied nations decided they needed to establish some ground rules and set up a monetary system, so more than 700 Allied representatives met at Bretton Woods, New Hampshire to create a plan. There they hammered out what they called (rather unimaginatively) the Bretton Woods Agreement. One of the major points of this document was to use the U.S. dollar as the main standard for converting all other currencies. It was also agreed,

Browsing at the Specialty Market

since everyone else had run out of it, that the U.S. dollar would remain the only currency backed by gold. Ultimately, the U.S. also ran out of gold, so in 1971, President Richard Nixon announced the end of Bretton Woods. Removal of this obstacle opened the door of the forex market to traders. The advent of Internet trading platforms has made it easy for investors to buy and sell and has transformed the market. It has gone from being where most exchanges are transactions to facilitate the purchase or sale of goods, to one where the main object is to make money from money.

When you hear investors talking about the forex market, it is a safe bet they are referring to the spot market, the place where currencies are bought and sold. Here is how it works: Currencies are traded in pairs, such as U.S. Dollars and Swiss Francs. The exchange rate is referred to as the "quote." The base currency is always equal to one monetary unit, which is usually the U.S. dollar. The quote currency is whatever you are buying and is the amount of that currency you can buy for one dollar. When your domestic (home) currency is the base currency, it is referred to as a direct quote. Suppose, for example, you want to buy Swiss francs and you see this quote:

$$USD/CHF = 1.22113$$

It means for every U.S. dollar you lay out, you will get 1.22 Swiss francs. When the opposite is true and the quoted currency is your home currency, it is referred to as an indirect quote. It would look like this:

$$CHF/USD = 0.818930$$

This means for every Swiss franc you lay out, you will get approximately eighty-two U.S. cents. When neither currency in the pair is your own, it is referred to as a cross currency. In all cases, the base currency is written on the left of the slash and the quote currency on the right. The base currency is the one in which the transaction is being made.

In addition to the quote, each currency pair has a bid (buy) price and an ask (sales) price. Suppose the bid price for Swiss francs is 1.22113 and the ask price is 1.22116. It would look like this:

$$USD/CHF = 1.22113/16$$

Investing Starting from Scratch

The spread between the bid price and the ask price is expressed as a *pip*. A pip is the smallest move the price can make and in this example, the difference is three pips. Forex brokers do not charge commissions, so they make their money from this spread. Pips may be tiny, but you will not hear the brokers complaining—remember we are talking about trillions of dollars trading daily.

Most currency fluctuations are infinitesimal—often less than a penny. So how do investors make money? The answer is low margin requirements and leverage, as much as 250-to-one. That means for every dollar you have in your account, you can control up to $250 in the market. In the forex market, vast fortunes have been won or lost on the smallest movements in price due to leverage.

Although every currency in the world is found in the marketplace, most of the trading involves just a handful of currencies: U.S. dollars, the Euro, British pounds, Swiss francs, and Japanese yen. Forex investors are avid consumers of information about economic trends in the countries involved and make money by focusing on fluctuating exchange and interest rates. Shopping strategies already familiar to us from the stock market are used in the forex market as well. Fundamental analysis is based on the same underlying theories, but instead of scrutinizing company financial statements, sales figures and management performance, the forex investor uses this method to analyze gross domestic product, employment statistics, interest rates, and political leadership. An investor using technical analysis uses charts to look for trends and is likely to use a sophisticated computer program that monitors slight changes between currency pairs. Technical analysis is the most commonly used strategy in forex trading.

> If you must play, decide upon three things at the start: the rules of the game, the stakes, and the quitting time.
> —Chinese Proverb

A Last Word of Caution

There are many successful investors who travel these avenues, but if you are not familiar with the terrain, you can lose your money as fast as I watched mine disappear in that slot machine. Think of it this way: if you have never scrambled an egg, you probably don't want to attempt a soufflé your first time in the kitchen. If anything in this specialty market looks appealing to you, come back when you are a seasoned investor.

THE BOTTOM LINE

- Hedge funds are small, actively-managed funds that focus on earning positive returns using a variety of investment strategies such as leverage, selling short and hedging with derivatives.
- Hedge funds are not regulated by the SEC.
- Most hedge funds are limited partnerships geared toward high net worth investors.
- Buying on margin is a strategy that uses leverage, or borrowed money, to purchase securities.
- Investors do not own the stock sold in a short sale—they borrow it. Long positions make money when the price of an asset goes up and short positions make money when the price of an asset goes down.
- The most common derivatives are futures contracts and options.
- Futures are based on predicting what commodity prices will be at designated dates.
- Options give you the *right* to buy or sell an underlying asset, but not the obligation.
- There are two types of options: calls and puts.
- Hedging is using options as a way to manage risk. Speculating is using options as a way to take advantage of short-term price fluctuations.
- The London Gold Pool resets the price of gold, known as the "Gold Fixing," daily.
- In the forex market, money is made on very small price movements using leverage.
- Forex traders use both fundamental and technical methods of analysis, but technical analysis is more common.

Investments and Financial Planning

"I retire on Friday and I haven't saved a dime. Here's your chance to become a legend!"

CHAPTER NINE

Guarding the Hens: Keeping the Fox Out of Your Henhouse

IF YOU HAVE READ THIS FAR, you are serious about taking charge of your own financial future. Please take a moment to congratulate yourself for taking a significant step in the right direction. You may also be feeling a little overwhelmed with all the decisions there are to make, but take heart—being responsible does not mean that you have to manage your chicken farm all by yourself. Often farmers find they sleep better at night after they have assembled a team of competent managers and hen keepers to help them select and guard their flocks.

Who are these people? Where do you find them and how do you decide which ones to add to your team? There are many types of professionals in the financial world, some with a whole alphabet of designations behind their names. We will decode these in the next section of this chapter, but first things first.

Before You Make an Appointment

Know What You Want

This point may sound silly, but the biggest financial blunder I have ever made was going to see a financial advisor unprepared. I let him talk me into putting money into something I didn't understand and consequently lost most of it—but at least I did gain some valuable experience. Before you make an appointment with anyone, decide exactly what kind of help you are seeking. Are you looking for assistance planning your whole investing strategy? Do you want your current portfolio reevaluated? Do you need another opinion on an investment you are considering? Or do you just have a tax-planning question that can be answered in one visit? Knowing what you want to accomplish is vital in selecting the right professional to help you. Imagine wandering into a design studio and giving a decorator carte blanche to redo your home any way she pleased. Or paying an architect to design and build your dream house by telling her, "Just do whatever you think is best." You would have definite ideas before you engaged these professionals, and a visit to a financial advisor is no different.

Check Them Out

The best way to find a prospective advisor is through personal recommendations. Ask your friends and family if they have someone they like, or check with co-workers or your human resources department at work. You can also browse professional websites that provide a list of their members in your area. Some good places to start your search are the National Association of Personal Financial Advisors (www.napfa.org), the Certified Financial Planner Board of Standards (www.cfp.net) and the Financial Planning Association (www.fpanet.org).

Don't hesitate to ask for client references from any professional you are considering. Talking to people who use her services will give you a better idea of the kind of work she does. You will also want to know if your candidate has ever faced disciplinary action for unlawful or unethical practices. Investment advisors are required to register with their state securities agencies or with the SEC. With either, they use Form ADV which has two parts. Part 1 contains information about their educational level, the amount of funds they are managing, and most importantly, any disciplinary action against them within the last ten years. Part 2 details their methods and fees. Registered advisors are only required to provide Part 2 to clients, but ask for both parts of Form ADV before you enter into a relationship. You may be able to find a copy of a registered advisor's Part 1 ADV online at the SEC website (www.sec.gov). To find your state securities regulator, log onto the North American Securities Administrator Association at www.nasaa.org or call 202-737-0900. If your planner is not registered with the state or the SEC, here are some other places to look:

- Certified Financial Planners Board of Standards has a "quick check tool" you can use to determine the planner's current certification status and if she has any public disciplinary history. Log onto their website at www.cfp.net or call 888-237-6275
- National Association of Insurance Commissioners allows you to search for complaints against insurance companies or their representatives. They are on the web at www.naic.org or call 816-842-3600.

Interview the Prospective Planner

A financial professional will typically offer a free introductory meeting to get acquainted and to determine if your needs are within her area of expertise. Take this opportunity to ask questions, such as how long she has been in the business, what types of financial planning she specializes in and about her investing philosophy. Do her answers fit your personal philosophy? What are her credentials? What kind of feeling do you get from talking with her? If you need help, there is an excellent—and extensive—checklist available on www.cfp.net to assist with your interviewing. Discussing your finances is a personal matter that should be treated with care and confidentiality, and it involves a great deal of trust. If you don't have positive feelings from your initial contact, keep looking until you find a better match.

Ask About Fees

Some financial professionals work as independent advisors and others work for banks, brokerages, or insurance companies. Some sell products and some do not, but they generally earn their income one of these ways:

- *By commission.* Professionals in this group earn their income from commissions when they complete transactions for you. They should evaluate your personal situation before making any investment recommendations. Since they act as both advisor and broker, there is a potential for conflict of interest; however, many investors prefer this arrangement because they get two services, but pay only one fee.
- *From fees.* Some fee-only professionals charge a fixed or hourly fee solely for their advice—they do not purchase or manage in-

vestments for you. Others earn their income through asset-based fees, which represent a percentage of your total portfolio under their watch. They may have a minimum portfolio requirement before they will accept you as a client. Asset-based fees have come under scrutiny lately, and it appears many financial professionals are moving away from them. They are opting instead for more customized billing methods, such as project fees or retainer fees.
- *By a combination of commissions and fees.* Fee-based planners earn money both through commissions on investment products they sell and from asset management or other fees.

The type you use will depend upon your needs and budget. The important point to remember is to ask your candidates up front how they are compensated and if they can give you an estimate of what your costs will be. Although you don't want to pay too much, this is probably not the best time to shop for bargains. A good advisor or planner who helps you structure a secure future can be worth her weight in gold. Interviewing several candidates should help you get an idea of a reasonable rate for services.

> Storefront financial experts are becoming so common that, if they were deer, local authorities would be tempted to stage a hunt to cull the herd.
>
> —JIM MCTAGUE

Assembling Your Financial Team

Anyone can hang out a shingle and call herself a financial advisor, wealth manager, investment consultant or any other creative title she chooses. This is why the interview process is such a crucial first step in finding someone who is truly qualified and who operates under a set of professional guidelines and a code of ethics. If you do business with an individual with no credentials, you will have no recourse in case of an ethical breach.

Investment advisors are in the business of giving advice about financial products, and some also manage portfolios. Financial planners take this one-step further. In addition to giving investment advice, they look at your big picture and can assist with goal-setting, retirement planning, tax issues, insurance requirements and estate planning. The best choice for you will vary by your specific needs. This is by no means an exhaustive list, but here are some of the professionals individual investors frequently engage:

Certified Financial Planners (CFP)

A CFP designation indicates the holder has successfully completed studies on over 100 topics including stocks, bonds, taxes, insurance and retirement and estate planning. They have passed a certification exam and met work experience standards. Their certification requires strict adherence to the CFP Board's code of ethics and continuing education requirements. Only professionals who have the CFP designation are allowed to call themselves financial planners.

Accredited Asset Management Specialist (AAMS)

This certification indicates the holder has completed a course of study and successfully passed an examination. Course work includes not only investing, but also insurance, tax issues and retirement planning. Continuing education is required to maintain this certification.

Certified Fund Specialists (CFS)

These professionals are experts in mutual funds. They advise their clients on which funds to choose and sometimes, if they are licensed, will buy and sell funds for them. Their certification requires continuing education to keep them current.

Certified Public Accountants (CPA)

CPAs are experts in accounting and tax issues and they may also be certified financial planners (CFPs). When they have the CFP certification, they can add to their financial planning knowledge base by getting a Personal Financial Specialist (PFS) designation from the American Institute of Certified Public Accountants. This makes them, in effect, a one-stop shop.

Chartered Financial Analyst (CFA)

The CFA designation is earned after completion of three exams and at least three years of qualified work experience. Holders of this credential are experts in economics and stock analysis. They pore over balance sheets, income statements, annual reports and press releases to make an educated prediction (i.e., guess) about how publicly-traded companies are going to perform. CFAs usually work for brokerage firms and not with individuals; however, I have included them in the list because these are the ones who advise other professionals what to buy and sell, and whose opinions appear on financial websites.

Chartered Financial Consultant (ChFC)

Similar to Certified Financial Planners, these professionals have passed extensive testing in the areas of financial planning, income tax, estate planning and insurance, and have a minimum of three years' relevant experience. They specialize in helping individuals analyze their personal situations and meet their financial goals.

Chartered Life Underwriter (CLU)

These are insurance professionals. This designation is awarded to those who have completed a program that includes pension planning, income tax, and estate planning as well as life insurance.

Chartered Retirement Planning Counselor (CRPC)

The specialty of a CRPC is estate planning and asset management during retirement. The American College for Financial Planning awards this designation to those who have completed approximately 100 hours of study and successfully passed an exam.

> Even if you have a good advisor, you still will want to become a knowledgeable investor. This way you can understand something about the markets and can have a dialogue with your team.
> —RAYMOND J. LUCIA

Some Caveats

Be very wary of any financial professional who makes claims about consistently "beating the market" or who guarantees a certain amount of return. In fact, using the word "guarantee" in reference to anything but annuities is illegal. No matter how competent they may be, no one can accurately predict the future. Also, watch out for those who don't listen to you or gloss over your wishes or concerns and insist they know what is best for you. Financial professionals should not act as substitutes for you, but as trusted partners. Do your due diligence, and you will not end up with a fox in your henhouse.

The Baskets

The rapidly disappearing defined benefit plans (pensions) provided a sense of security to yesterday's employees. Their employers made all the investing decisions for them and the employees knew exactly what their benefits were going to be when they retired. Everything was nice and secure—that is, unless you happened to work for a company who hit the financial rocks and stopped funding their pensions. Defined contribution plans, on the other hand, sit squarely on the individual's shoulders. Some employers will match employee contributions up to a designated amount, but the responsibility of how that money is invested is left entirely up to the worker. Scary? Not for you, because you have made the important and wise decision to seize control of your financial future. At this point you have learned how to make a plan, how to sort out the different types of investments, who you can ask for advice and how to make purchases. Now, it is time to decide what kinds of baskets you need for your eggs and who is going to store them for you.

Types of Baskets

401(k) PLANS—TAX-DEFERRED

A 401(k) is a qualified plan offered through an employer. Each pay period, an amount you designate is deducted from your paycheck and deposited to an account held in your name. In a best-case scenario, your employer matches your contribution. Since the deduction is made before income taxes are calculated, you can make a significant contribution and hardly notice it on your paycheck. This means money you would ordinarily pay to Uncle Sam is working for you instead. You will not pay income tax on your contributions and the earnings on them until you make withdrawals. Penalties will apply if you dip into your 401(k) before retirement age (with a few exceptions). The IRS has established contribution limits, and sometimes the plans have their own caps. Most plans allow participants to choose their own investments from a pool of products, but some employers hire professionals to make the investment selections.

THE ROTH 401(k)

Introduced in January 2006, this follows the same rules as a regular 401(k) plan, except it is funded with after-tax money. This takes a bigger bite out of your paycheck's bottom line, but all those earnings accumulate tax-free—forever. You can withdraw funds from Roth plans without penalty at age 59½, provided the account is at least five years old. You can withdraw your principal at any time without penalty; only the earnings are subject to penalties.

Before we go on to the next type of basket, I want to point out some pitfalls on the road to financial freedom. I know I said I was not going to give any advice in this book, but there are two mistakes so common with 401(k)s, I would be remiss if I didn't mention them:

Mistake #1: Holding too much employer stock

As of this writing, there are no governmental restrictions on the amount of 401(k) assets that can be held in company stock. Since contributions made by an employer often come in the form of company stock, it is easy to become over-weighted in that one asset. Although it is a wonderful thing to have faith in your company, most professionals recommend holding no more than ten to twenty percent of company stock in your retirement portfolio. The people at Enron can vouch for this wisdom.

Mistake #2: Borrowing from your future

Many 401(k) plans have the option for participants to take loans, but don't do it. Even if the interest rates are lower than another type of loan, it will cost you dearly in lost earnings. Taking money out of your 401(k) should only be done for the direst of circumstances and after all other possibilities have been exhausted. If this is your only option, then you are almost certainly living above your means and I encourage you to go directly to Chapters Twelve and Thirteen. That said, back to the baskets...

403(b) PLANS

A 403(b) is very similar to a 401(k) except it is only available to employees of certain tax-exempt organizations such as churches, colleges, libraries, and some non-profit institutions. One major difference is 403(b) plans do not allow participants to invest in individual stocks. Instead, contributions are invested in annuities through insurance companies or in specified mutual funds. You may hear this plan referred to as a tax-sheltered annuity (TSA) or a tax-deferred annuity (TDA) because originally annuities were the only choice.

Guarding the Hens: Keeping the Fox Out of Your Henhouse

Mutual funds held outside annuities were added as an investment option to the 403(b) in 1974, but the former names linger on.

ROTH 403(b) PLANS

Like the Roth 401(k), these plans also made their debut in January 2006. The difference between this plan and a regular 403(b) is contributions are made with after-tax dollars. As with any other type of Roth account, you can withdraw funds without penalty at age 59½, provided the account is at least five years old. You can withdraw your principal at any time without penalty; only the earnings are subject to penalties.

TRADITIONAL IRAS

Contributions to a traditional IRA may be tax deductible, depending on your income, and earnings grow on a tax-deferred basis. The theory is that later, when you need to make withdrawals, you will be in a lower tax bracket. Although that may or may not be the case, IRA contributions are a good thing, especially if your employer doesn't offer a retirement plan. And if you should find yourself in the fortunate position of maxing out your employer's plan, you can make contributions to an IRA in addition to a retirement plan at work.

In order to establish an IRA, you must have earned income (as opposed to passive income from rentals, investments, or other pursuits). You can contribute at any time during the tax year up to a limit specified by the IRS. There is a substantial penalty for taking early withdrawals, although there are some exceptions. There is also an age established by the IRS where you *must* start making withdrawals and that is currently 70½ years. Uncle Sam is patient, but he is not going to wait forever to get his taxes.

ROTH IRA

Contributions to a Roth IRA are made with after-tax dollars and are not tax-deductible, but like the Roth 401(k) and Roth 403(b), all earnings are tax-exempt. There is no mandatory withdrawal age—you can take distributions as early as age 59½ as long as the account has been in existence for at least five years. If for some reason you do not need the money, you can pass Roths intact to your heirs. Not everyone is eligible to open a Roth account because there are income limitations. Currently an individual cannot have an adjusted gross income of more than $114,000 annually and a couple cannot exceed

$166,000. You can convert your traditional IRA to a Roth, but you must pay taxes on the current account balance first.

Simplified Employee Pension– SEP

The SEP IRA is often used by small employers or people who are self-employed. Contributions are discretionary up to certain limits and the employer (or you) gets to take a tax deduction for contributions. The employee (or you) does not pay taxes until withdrawal time. Another bonus: the employee (or you) can also make a traditional IRA contribution. So what does all this mean? If you are self-employed and want to sock away as much as you can, the SEP will allow you to contribute as much as twenty-five percent of your income up to a maximum of $49,000 (in 2009.) There are, of course, rules and regulations, but if this shoe looks like it might fit, try it on.

> Nobody on Wall Street has a monopoly on truth. Market strategists don't. Money managers and investment-newsletter writers don't. Brokers, financial planners and insurance agents don't. Newspaper columnists most certainly don't. So treat all financial advice with caution. Look at every investment and every investment strategy with profound skepticism. Think long and hard about every financial myth. If you do that, you will do just fine.
> —Jonathon Clements

Who Will Hold Your Baskets?

Your employer will select the custodian for 401(k) and 403(b) plans. You hope they will select one that allows you plenty of investment choices. You can open an IRA account at just about any financial institution including brokerage firms, banks, and insurance companies. To keep things simple, you may want to consider consolidating to one or two custodians. Some things to consider when you are making your selection:

1. What is their fee structure?
2. What is your impression of their customer service?
3. Are the statements easy to read?
4. Is there a physical location where you can speak to someone face-to-face?

5. Are they online? If so, can you download statements and forms? How is their technical support?
6. What investment choices do they offer?

The last consideration is especially important if you want maximum flexibility in your investing. Some custodians limit your choices to their line of investment products; at the other end of the spectrum is the institution where you have almost unlimited choices and make all the decisions. A few custodians offer self-directed IRAs that allow you to hold any asset allowed by the IRS in your account, including real estate.

Another word about those statements: read them. If you don't understand them, call your advisor or customer service representative and keep her on the phone until you do. Don't be intimidated—it's your future.

THE BOTTOM LINE

- Before you make an appointment with a financial professional, it is important to decide exactly what kind of help you are seeking.
- Ask for references and check for disciplinary actions against any financial professional you are considering.
- Ask questions of your advisor. If you don't feel comfortable with her, keep looking.
- Financial professionals may earn money from commissions, fees or a combination of the two.
- Anyone can call herself an investment advisor. Use the interview process to choose an advisor that is truly a professional.
- Be very wary of any financial professional who makes claims about consistently beating the market or who guarantees a certain amount of return.
- 401(k) Plans and 403(b) plans are only offered through employers.
- IRA plans and SEP plans can be opened by individuals with earned income.
- Roth plans are funded by after-tax dollars, and all earnings are tax-exempt if the account is held for at least five years.

CHAPTER TEN

Keeping Track of Egg Production

WHEN YOUR HENHOUSE IS POPULATED, you will begin receiving small mountains of mail from the various mutual fund companies, insurance companies, banks and brokerage firms that are holding your baskets. After you have read them—something you now know how to do—you will want to compile all that information in one place so you can have a good, overall picture of your progress as an egg farmer. You can keep records any way that suits you, but regardless of your method, you will need to know these three basic things:

1. What kinds of hens do you own?
2. How are they laying?
3. How much room are they taking up in your henhouse?

> However beautiful the strategy, you should occasionally look at the results.
> —WINSTON CHURCHILL

What Kinds of Hens Do You Own?

The IRS requires you to keep good records of each hen you buy or sell. The reason they expect you to know your *cost basis* of any stock or mutual fund you own is so they can relieve you of their share of your profit when you sell something. This is simply a matter of keeping up with these few facts:

- Date of purchase
- The number of shares or units purchased

- Price paid for each share or unit
- Commissions or fees paid
- Dividends or interest received
- Date sold
- Price received for each share or unit

Having this information allows you to track your capital gains and losses. After meeting this requirement, you can make your records as simple or as complex as you want them to be.

> But in this world nothing can be said to be certain, except death and taxes.
> —BENJAMIN FRANKLIN

How the Hens Are Laying: Measuring Returns

A *rate of return* is the value of an investment at the beginning of a period of time compared to the value of the investment at the end of that period expressed as a percentage. It measures how much was gained or lost relative to how much was risked. Here's an example:

Last year, Ima Investor invested $1,000 in a stock. A little more than one year later, she sold it for $1,150, which means she realized a gain of $150. To find the return on her investment, she divides the amount of her dollar return by the amount of the original investment. Multiply the fraction that results by 100 to convert it to a percentage. Here are Ima's calculations:

$$\$150/1000 = .15 \times 100 = 15\%$$

Why is this number important to her? She knows she made $150—why not just calculate her returns in dollar value? Expressing returns as ratios instead of amounts offers several advantages:
- Ratios are unchanged regardless of the dollar amount. Her rate of return is the same whether she invested $100, $1,000, or even $1 million.
- Ratios allow her to compare returns between different types of hens who lay on different schedules (time periods).
- Ratios enable her to compare her returns year after year. If the same investment earns ten percent this year, but only eight percent the next, she may decide to sell off unproductive hens.

Keeping Track of Egg Production

- Ratios make it easy for her to calculate estimated returns on investments she is considering for purchase. For example, Ima has $1,000 to invest and estimates a return of eleven percent annually. She wants to know how much she would have at the end of one year at that rate, so she multiplies the investment amount by the rate of anticipated return to arrive at her accumulated value. Her calculation looks like this:

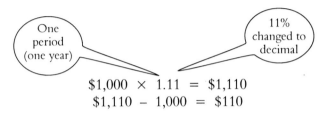

The number one represents one period, in this case a year, and the percentage was converted back to a decimal. She sees she will make a gain of $110 if the rate of return rate doesn't change.

Ima can also calculate returns on the investments she holds—the faithful layers that roost in her henhouse year after year. To do this, she uses the market value at the beginning of each period, just as if she were buying the investment, and the market value at the end of each period, just as if she were selling it. This result is called an "unrealized" gain or loss.

The gains (or losses) from each period are added (or subtracted), which increases (or decreases) her total principal invested. This tells Ima her accumulated value each period. If in the unlikely event an investment were to make exactly the same dollar return year after year, the rate of return would decrease because the principal amount has increased due to reinvested earnings. Say, for example, Ima bought a new hen for $1,000. By the end of the first year, the hen had produced 150 eggs ($150), a return of fifteen percent. At the end of the second year, the hen again produced 150 eggs ($150), which is a decrease of two percent from the first year. Why? Because the invested principal at the beginning of the second year was $1,150. Here is the math:

$$\$150/\$1,150 = .13 \times 100 = 13\%$$

Don't worry. You will not usually have to work through figures

> Even though you are on the right track, you will get run over if you just sit there.
> —Will Rogers

like this. In most cases, your basket holders will do them for you—that's what is in the mountain of papers they send. But now that you know how it's done, those statements will no longer be such a mystery.

Tracking Tools

Online

There are numerous websites that offer free portfolio tracking services, and many also offer tools for analysis and planning. If there is a stock you have your eye on, you can add it to a watch list. The minute it goes on sale (i.e., is at or below your desired buy price), you will receive an e-mail letting you know. If you have an account at a brokerage firm, you will almost always find these services on their website as well. Here are a few of the better-known sites to check out:

- www.smartmoney.com/tools
- www.finance.yahoo.com
- www.quicken.com
- www.moneycentral.com
- www.zacks.com
- www.morningstar.com

Morningstar is one of the best-known and most widely used websites for investing information. You can keep your portfolio as well as a watch list there and get quotes on stock, ratings on mutual funds and quite a bit of other free information. They offer a premium membership for $159 per year at the time of this writing. Among other benefits, such as access to analyst's reports and opinions, membership allows you to use their "Portfolio X-Ray" feature, which provides an analysis of your portfolio that tells you everything you could ever want to know. For example, it analyzes the amount of risk you are taking, and classifies holdings by sector, region, and style. It tells you how much of a stock you really own, including shares held in mutual funds. It compares your holdings to the appropriate benchmark index and makes recommendations for changes. It tells you who your top ten producers are and makes suggestions for rebalancing your portfolio, and offers lots of "what if" scenarios to help

Keeping Track of Egg Production

you reach your goals. You get the idea. Each website is a little different, so browse through them to see if there is one that is a good fit for your needs.

Sometimes the amount of information offered online seems overwhelming. Don't let this discourage you. Remember, you are in control and stay true to your own style. If the whole idea of this much analysis makes you queasy, just go with easy-does-it mutual funds or index funds. Nobody says you have to buy individual stocks. Or perhaps you are a little squeamish about putting all that personal information into cyberspace, PIN or no PIN. No problem—there are other good options.

Software

QUICKEN®

Quicken® is a financial management software program that covers all the bases. The "Cash Flow Center" tracks all of your income and expenses. You can reconcile your bank and credit card accounts and pay bills online. It has the capability to download your transactions from most banks, brokerage firms, and credit card companies in one-step. There are many options for tracking and budgeting, and a handy "find" feature that allows you to go instantly to specific transactions. In the "Property and Debt Center" you can record all your other assets, from your house to Great Aunt Martha's diamond brooch—anything you consider of value. In fact, you can keep the inventory of your entire house there, as well as records of your insurance policies and other important papers if you are so inclined. This is also the section for entering mortgages, car notes and any other long-term debts you may have.

The "Investing Center" allows you to track your investment performances (how the hens are laying) and see which hens are the best producers and the worst producers. It has features that will estimate capital gains, help you rebalance your portfolio and keep up with your progress toward your personal financial goals. You can also access www.quicken.com, which connects you to many investment research sites that will provide more information than you probably want to know.

Having everything in one place allows you to check your net worth with a couple of clicks anytime you care to look. It also simplifies income tax preparation. The tax reports feature is a big time saver when it is time to gather records, or you can integrate your information with Turbo Tax. Lest I sound like an advertiser for Quicken®, let me assure you I have no connection with Intuit, the software company that markets it. Microsoft® Money is another excellent program and there are other software choices available—Quicken® is just my personal choice for pick of the litter.

Quicken® and Microsoft® Money have both been around quite awhile—in computer-world terms—and new software is coming on the market constantly. When I Googled "portfolio tracking software," I got thousands of hits, so you can shop around. Alternatively, you can create your own system with a spreadsheet.

EXCEL

If you have Excel on your computer, you can download a portfolio template from Microsoft Office Online. Log onto www.office.microsoft.com or from Excel and type *Portfolio Tracking* in the search box. There are a number of forms you can choose, from simple to very complex, or just use them as a guide to create your own custom form.

Who Needs Software?

No computer? No problem. Columnar pads still work exactly the same way they always have. All you need is a pencil and a calculator and you are good to go. You can design your own or copy one of the Excel examples. And yes, I do know very successful investors who still prefer this method.

> Simplicity, simplicity, simplicity! I say, let your affairs be as two or three, and not a hundred or a thousand; instead of a million count half a dozen, and keep your accounts on your thumbnail.
> —HENRY DAVID THOREAU

Maintaining Harmony in the Henhouse

From time to time, you will need to take a walk through your henhouse to make sure things are operating according to your master plan. Are your hens occupying their allotted space? Or have they crowded out some of their less aggressive sisters? If you find that is the case, it is time to move them back where they belong. This is what is meant by rebalancing your portfolio. In order to do this, you simply sell off some of the more prodigious producers, the investment that is over your target allocation, and use that money to buy more of the investments that are under your target allocation. You are probably asking, "Why would I want to sell off investments that are producing above average results and buy more of those that aren't?" That was *my* first question, anyway, and there are two reasons why you would want to do this. First, you will be buying low and selling high, and that is certainly preferable to the other way around. More importantly, rebalancing is the way you will get your portfolio back to its original design so you can sleep at night knowing you are adequately diversified. You don't want one asset to grow so large that if it tanked, you would lose a big part of your portfolio. Once you get things established, you should only have to do this about once a year. In the beginning, though, you will probably want to check every quarter or so. If your investments include mutual funds, you will need to know what types of securities each one holds in order to assess your allocations correctly. In addition, if you decide to buy individual stocks—and this is certainly optional—you will need to know the allocation of each stock in your total portfolio so you will not depend too much on one producer.

Think of rebalancing as routine maintenance. It reduces your risk by keeping you diversified, thus providing better long-term returns. Additionally, as we grow older or our circumstances change, our tolerance for risk may change. Rebalancing annually provides the opportunity to reassess your personal situation. Remember that you can redesign your henhouse any time you want. It can be expanded, remodeled or torn down and rebuilt as your needs change.

> Organizing is what you do before you do something, so that when you do it, it is not all mixed up.
> —A. A. MILNE

Financial Housekeeping

Since you have decided to get your finances in order, now is a good time to organize and update all the other important papers related to your affairs too. Here are the ones on the must-have list:

INVESTING STARTING FROM SCRATCH

Will

First, make sure you have one—that is, unless you want to leave all your hard-won gains to Uncle Sam. Second, let your executor or executrix know where it is. Do not store it in a safety deposit box unless you are sure someone can get into it after your death. A will doesn't have to be complicated, but I don't recommend a do-it-yourself-off-the-internet job; this is a task best left to the professionals. If you make a mistake, there are no do-overs after you are gone.

Durable Power of Attorney

A durable power of attorney gives legal authority to another person to make financial and legal decisions for you if you should become incapable of managing your own affairs. This is not a responsibility to take lightly, so make sure you have thought it through carefully. Give it to the person you have designated to act in this capacity for you and keep a copy for yourself.

Power of Attorney for Health Care

The person you designate as power of attorney for your health care gives—or withholds—consent for treatment if you are unable to do so. This has to be someone you trust with your life, so make sure you also entrust them with the document. Remember to keep a copy for yourself.

Advance Health Care Directive (Living Will)

A living will designates your wishes for medical care or treatment if you should become unable to give your own consent. Make copies for the people who would be involved in case of your incapacity, including your doctor. Also, discuss your wishes with all of them in advance so you can make sure everyone is on the same page.

If you have not attended to any of these documents yet, your attorney can take care of all of them in one visit.

Life Insurance

Make sure your executor or executrix knows where your policy is kept. As with your will, do not store your insurance policy in your safety deposit box unless you are sure it can be accessed if you should die.

It is desirable to keep these important papers stored

> Life is what happens to you while you're busy making other plans.
> —John Lennon

Keeping Track of Egg Production

in a fireproof safe. If that is not possible, keep copies of them in your safety deposit box so you will be able to secure replacements in case of disaster. What else can you keep in your safety deposit box? Deeds, titles, proof of paid-off-loans and copies of all your other types of insurance policies. If you have something very valuable—jewelry, art, or antiques, for example—keep any associated receipts or appraisals. It is also a good idea to keep a list of account numbers with issuer contact information—this can come in very handy in case of theft or loss. If you use a program like Quicken®, you can store everything on a CD. Once a year when you rebalance your portfolio, update your list or CD and the housekeeping is done. The idea is to make settling your affairs as uncomplicated as possible. Leaving things in good order is the last thoughtful deed you can do for your heirs.

THE BOTTOM LINE

- The IRS requires investors to keep careful records of each investment bought and sold in order to track capital gains and losses.
- A rate of return is the value of an investment at the beginning of a period of time. compared to the value of the investment at the end of that period expressed as a percentage.
- An unrealized gain or loss is computed on investments that are held in the portfolio.
- Portfolio tracking may be done online, with money management software or by hand.
- Periodic rebalancing of a portfolio helps ensure adequate diversification.
- Documents that are important to have include a will, durable power of attorney, power of attorney for health care, and advance health care directive (living will).
- Discuss the location of important documents with the people entrusted with carrying out your wishes.
- Financial housekeeping is a gift to your heirs.

> Good fortune is what happens when opportunity meets with planning.
> —THOMAS EDISON

"After federal, state, and local taxes, you get one-third of a wish."

CHAPTER ELEVEN

Selling Your Eggs

THE TRADITIONAL CONCEPT OF RETIREMENT is fading into history as more and more of us are remaining in the work force long past age sixty-five. Some are opting to work part-time as a way to stay busy and involved. Others, even though they can afford to retire early, continue to work because they need health insurance coverage. Many of us simply cannot afford to retire, but we may redefine ourselves by starting new careers, perhaps turning an avocation into a vocation. Even those who do not have to earn income are finding activities that add meaning to their lives. The days of just passing time with shuffleboard and bridge are over. The good news for Boomers who wish to continue working is that they will soon be hot properties. As the younger workforce shrinks, competition for older workers will become more intense. It's clear that corporate America has begun to recognize where the action is. Have you noticed the commercials lately? Did you ever think you would hear Led Zeppelin in the background of a television commercial? Or Bob Dylan piped into an elevator? The times they are definitely a changin'.

> Age is only a number, a cipher for the records. A man can't retire his experience. He must use it.
> —BERNARD BARUCH

Transitioning into Retirement

Whether you use your retirement savings as supplementary income or depend on these funds for a large part of your support, it will be necessary to do some planning. You will now be creating your own paychecks or "income streams." Some will flow from sources such as pensions and Social Security payments, so one decision you will need to make is when to apply for these benefits. This is especially crucial if you plan to continue working. The earliest you can apply for Social Security is age sixty-two, but if you have not reached full retirement age as defined by the Social Security Administration, your benefits check will be reduced by one dollar for every two dollars you earn above the annual allowed limit. The Senior Citizens Freedom to Work Act of 2000 ended this penalty for people who reach full retirement age. If you wait until you reach that magic number, you can earn as much as you want with no reduction in benefits. Log onto www.socialsecurity.gov for current limits and a wealth of information, or you can do it the old-fashioned way and pay a visit to your nearest Social Security office.

If you are fortunate enough to have a pension from your employer, your human resources (HR) department should be able to answer your questions about applying for these benefits. The most important thing to remember about these sources is there are no do-overs. You only get to choose how and when you will receive benefits once. Do your research and find out everything you need to know before you start taking payouts. If you don't understand the implications of the various options available, keep asking until you do. Still another income stream will be created from tapping into your savings—taking those golden eggs to market at last.

> The question isn't at what age I want to retire, it's at what income.
> —GEORGE FOREMAN

Selling Your Golden Eggs

Some of us are interested in leaving a legacy or a large inheritance to our heirs and we want to hold on to as many of our eggs as possible. Others of us simply want to know how much we can afford to spend and how many eggs we can sell. In my research, I found a lot of advice on how to put your money *into* savings and investments, but finding information on how to get your money out was a different story. There are two main concerns here:

1. How do you protect your nest eggs? It would be a shame to go

through years of carefully tending your hens just to give your beautiful golden eggs to the government.
2. How can you make sure your supply of eggs doesn't expire before you do?

Although they had vastly different ideas of how it should look when you are finished, almost every advisor's book I read recommended doing some remodeling of your henhouse when you near retirement age. You will probably want to replace some of those temperamental growth stock hens with more placid bond, REIT and income stock hens. These predictable producers will assume a more prominent place in your henhouse so you can have easy access to their eggs. You will also want to keep a cash pool equal to a year or two (some say more) of expenses. As a rule of thumb, many financial advisors advocate withdrawing no more than four percent annually from your portfolio to minimize the risk of outliving your assets. In lean years, when the hens are not producing as well, you will have to either adjust your spending or find a way to increase your income.

Your individual tax situation will determine which baskets to sell from first, but usually it is from the taxable accounts. This would be a good time to enlist the services of a financial team—even if it is for nothing more than to show them your plan and get a second opinion. It is also a good time to review your will and insurance policies. Make it a practice to review your important documents annually and keep your beneficiaries up-to-date. There has been more than one horror story about an unintended person (such as an ex-husband) receiving a windfall because the deceased neglected to change her beneficiary.

> We'll try to cooperate fully with the IRS, because, as citizens, we feel a strong patriotic duty not to go to jail.
> —DAVE BARRY

The RBD and the RMD for Your IRA According to the IRS

Time to translate a little government speak. RBD stands for *Required Beginning Date*, the day when you must begin taking RMD or *Required Minimum Distributions* from your IRA. The required beginning date is April 1 following the calendar year you reach age seventy-and-one-half. The key word here is *following*. This means if your seventieth birthday rolls around between January 1 and June 30, you will turn seventy and one-half in the same year and your RBD will be April 1 of the next year. If your birthday falls between July 1 and December 31, you will not be seventy and one-half until the next year, so your RBD will be April 1 of the year after that. (They couldn't just make it easy and set it at seventy, could they?) This rule applies to traditional, SEP and SIMPLE IRAs. The rules do not apply to Roth IRA owners because they are not required to take distributions, but they do apply to Roth beneficiaries. So much for the when.

The "how much factor" (RMD) is based on your life expectancy. The IRS provides tables that will supply this information for you. You simply divide the fair market value of your account by the factor from the IRS table and withdraw that amount. Your withdrawals are taxed at your ordinary income tax rate. After the first year, your RMD must be taken out by December 31 each year. Your IRA custodian is required to notify you when a distribution is due, and although they are not required to provide you with the amount due, most will if you ask.

The IRS will only wait so long for its tax money and is not amused if you don't handle this in a timely manner. If you do not take your RMD, you will be socked with a penalty of fifty percent of what you should have withdrawn but did not. And don't think they'll forget about the ordinary income tax on the distribution, either.

Making Your Savings Last As Long As You Do with Annuities

All the calculations in the world will be meaningless if you live twenty or thirty years longer than anticipated. If this is a real concern for you and you fear you might run out of money when you can least afford to, you might want to consider an *annuity*. Annuities are contracts sold by insurance companies that may include a choice of death benefits, but they are not

> Retirement is like a long vacation in Vegas. The goal is to enjoy it the fullest, but not so fully that you run out of money.
> —JONATHAN CLEMENTS

life insurance policies. Life insurance is designed to cover you in case you die; annuities are designed to cover you in case you live. The concept, in a nutshell, is you pay a sum of money to an insurance company, and they in turn promise to pay you an income stream for the rest of your life or for a specified time period. There are two phases to annuities: the accumulation phase—where you pay into them—and the payout phase—where they pay out to you. Depending on the type of annuity, the payout phase can start immediately or it can be deferred to a future date. The income earned in an annuity is tax deferred, which means no taxes are due on gains until the income is withdrawn.

Deciphering the insurance jargon and understanding how annuities work can be quite a challenge. Let's start by breaking them down into the three basic types:

1. A *fixed annuity* is usually purchased with a single premium payment. Very much like a CD, the premium you pay is deposited to an account that earns a rate of interest guaranteed by the insurance company. A fixed annuity is the most conservative type. The risk of market fluctuations is eliminated, but alas, so is the potential for larger gains. Because the returns for fixed annuities are straightforward, there are no sales and management fees attached. It is important to note that "fixed" is a relative term and the insurance company gets to make the rules. If you purchase this type of annuity, make sure you understand when and how interest rates can be changed.
2. *Variable annuities* may be purchased with one or more premium payments that are invested in one of the insurance company's investment subaccounts. Subaccounts are similar to mutual funds and may be composed of stocks, bonds, or other securities. Returns from variable annuities fluctuate with the market depending on the underlying investment performance—that means your payouts will not always be the same. Also, since there is active management involved, there will be more layers of fees that can have a significant impact on your returns.
3. An *equity-indexed annuity* is something of a hybrid product. An equity-indexed annuity is basically a fixed annuity with the added feature of additional earnings from stock market returns based on changes in a selected index such as the S&P 500.

Probably the most concise explanation of the differences among the three investing options is this:

- Fixed annuities are designed for saving
- Variable annuities are designed for investing
- Equity indexed annuities are a combination of both

Putting Money In

DEFERRED ANNUITIES

Deferred annuities are often referred to as savings annuities and are usually funded with contributions made over a long period of time. Annuities are designed as retirement vehicles and can be part of either qualified or non-qualified plans. *Qualified plans* are subject to the rules of the IRS regarding retirement accounts. For example, they are funded with pre-tax dollars and there are limits on maximum contributions in any one year. The IRS determines the age when you must take distributions (currently age seventy and one-half) and the age where you must not without incurring a penalty (currently before age fifty-nine and one-half). In addition to IRS penalties, the insurance company may impose surrender charges for early withdrawals.

Non-qualified plans are funded with after-tax dollars, so there are no limits on maximum contributions. Often people use non-qualified plans to sock away additional savings when they have reached the limits on their qualified plans. In either case, earnings grow tax-deferred until you start taking distributions.

Death benefits vary among companies, but they typically provide insurance protection up to the point of annuitization, i.e., payouts begin. That means if you should die before receiving your first payment, the insurance company guarantees to return the premiums you have paid to your beneficiaries.

IMMEDIATE ANNUITIES

As its name implies, an immediate annuity begins making payouts immediately—usually within thirty days—after you make your investment. You typically fund these annuities with a single, lump sum payment. Where do you get that lump? The most common source is rollovers from qualified plans such as 401(k)s or 403(b)s.

Selling Your Eggs

Other possibilities are proceeds from downsizing, matured bonds, inheritances, sales of assets, or hitting it big in Vegas (just kidding about that last one). You can even exchange a life insurance policy with cash value for an annuity using something called a 1035 exchange. In an immediate annuity, someone else manages your investments and you get to sleep well knowing a check will arrive in your mailbox every month, guaranteed. For how long? That depends on the payout option you choose, and there are many.

> I advise you to go on living solely to enrage those who are paying your annuities. It is the only pleasure I have left.
> —VOLTAIRE

Taking Money Out

The option you select will determine the amount and duration of your payouts and there are multiple variations of these depending on the issuer. You will find the terms *single life* or *lifetime income, joint and survivor* and *period certain* in a myriad of combinations. Here are some examples:

- *Single life*: You will receive payouts monthly for the rest of your life; they stop upon your death. If you have put in more than you have taken out, well, that's life—or in this case, the absence of it. Your beneficiary gets nothing, but the insurance company is happy.
- *Single life with period certain*: You will receive payouts for the rest of your life, with the added proviso that you get to choose a set number of years for payouts. If you should die prematurely, payouts will continue to your beneficiary for the selected number of years.
- *Single life installment refund*: You will receive payouts as long as you live. If you die before you have received an amount equal to what you put in (your premium), payouts will continue to your beneficiary until the total paid (to you and the beneficiary) equals your initial premiums.
- *Single life with cash refund*: This is the same idea as the single life installment refund option, except that the difference is paid to your beneficiary in a lump sum.
- *Period certain*: Payouts are guaranteed for a designated number of years, so this means you could outlive your annuity. If you

should die prematurely, payouts continue to your beneficiary until the end of the period.
- *Joint and survivor, 100%*: Payouts are made as long as both you and your joint annuitant are living. When one of you dies, the other continues to receive the full benefit. This is most often used by couples.
- *Joint and survivor, 75%, 50%, first or either*: When one annuitant dies, payouts are reduced to the survivor by a specified percentage. Why would you do this? Because payouts are higher than with the 100% option as long as both of you are living.
- *Joint and survivor, 75%, 50%, only primary*: Payouts are reduced by the specified percentage only if the primary annuitant dies. If the contingent annuitant dies first, nothing changes. A couple might use this when the primary annuitant is the partner most in need of income.

You can also access your money by taking lump sums, partial payments or scheduled payments. The most important thing to remember about annuitizing your contract (beginning to receive payouts) is this: Once payouts start, your decisions are irreversible. Also, the life insurance benefit usually stops unless you have taken an option for it to continue. The more whistles and bells attached, i.e., the more contingencies involved, the lower the monthly payout. As you would with any contract, read the fine print carefully and make sure you fully understand before you sign on the dotted line. If you want to know how much you would have to deposit to receive your desired amount of money each month, there is a handy calculator on www.immediateannuities.com.

Whistles and Bells

We already know the value of a variable annuity goes up and down with the market. If you were to die prematurely while it is in a slump, the regular death benefit would be a good deal. But what if the market is at a peak? If your beneficiaries received the death benefit, they would lose out on all that gain. An optional stepped-up death benefit will return either your premiums paid or the value of your account, whichever is higher. There are a number of ways to calculate investment gains—still another choice to make. Annuities are complex and vary by the company that issues them. If you think these products may be a good option for you, please consider getting some help from an objective advisor to help you look at them from every angle.

Tax Considerations

The portion of your payment subject to income tax depends on whether the annuity is held in a qualified or non-qualified plan and if it is fixed or variable. If your annuities are qualified plans, you pay tax on every penny you withdraw because your contributions were made with pre-tax dollars. This is true whether the annuity is fixed or variable.

If a fixed annuity is held in a non-qualified plan, part of the payment is principal and part is interest. Only the interest is taxed because you have already paid tax on the principal (your initial investment). The income from variable annuities comes from gains made in the markets. You are taxed only on these gains for variable annuities held in non-qualified plans.

Something to Think About

The taxable portion of payouts you receive from an annuity are taxed as ordinary income at your individual tax rate. When you make long-term gains (assets held over a year) in a mutual fund, you are taxed at the capital gains rate. Currently, in 2009, the highest capital gains tax rate is fifteen percent while the highest individual tax rate is thirty-five percent. This extra twenty percent tax rate is usually the biggest criticism of variable annuities by experts.

Another criticism of annuities is that they have no step-up basis like other investments. Here is what that means: Let's say your Aunt Agnes has left you a mutual fund in which she invested $50,000. Because she did her homework and chose well, at the time of her death and your inheritance, it has a value of $100,000. The IRS does not make you pay taxes on the $50,000 gain. The cost basis is stepped up to $100,000 and that becomes the starting point for taxation of any future gains you make. If Aunt Agnes had purchased a $50,000 annuity instead and it had doubled in value, you would have to pay ordinary income tax on the $50,000 gain—bummer.

Safeguards: Make Sure They Make the Grade

Sellers of annuities are overseen by their state insurance commissions. In addition, variable annuity products are regulated by the SEC and/or FINRA. Despite this, it is important to remember any guarantee is only as strong as the company that stands behind it. There are independent companies, which rate insurance companies, and it is highly recommended you check out any company you are considering doing business with. Try these sites for ratings: A.M. Best www.ambest.com (look for A- or better), Standard & Poor's www.standardandpoors.com (look for AA or better) and Weiss Research www.weissratings.com.

One Last Word of Caution

If you have ever tried to read an insurance contract, you probably found the language complex, esoteric and sometimes archaic. You probably gave up somewhere before the end and just trusted the insurance agent to translate it for you. This is not your car we are talking about here—this is the rest of your life. I cannot stress enough how important it is to make sure you understand everything about the contract before you sign on the bottom line. Annuities can be an excellent investment depending on your situation. Most people invest in them for the death benefit, tax deferral and various kinds of guarantees, and these come with a price. You should know the commission paid to sellers of annuities is one of the highest of all investment products, so it is equally important that you trust your advisor.

Reverse Mortgages

If your house is your greatest asset, you belong to a large club because this is true for many Americans. If you have owned it a long time, it has probably appreciated in value and you have quite a bit of equity or ownership. It is lovely when the mortgage is paid off and the house payments stop, but unfortunately, the expenses never do. Repairs, property taxes and skyrocketing insurance rates can consume quite a big chunk of your monthly budget. One solution is to sell your home, take the tidy profit, and move to less expensive digs. But what if you don't want to move? You can let your house pay you for a change with a *reverse mortgage*.

A reverse mortgage is a loan against the value of your home that you do not have to repay as long as you live there. Here is how it works: To be eligible, you must be at least sixty-two years old. You must own your home, but it does not have to be free and clear. If you still have a mortgage, you can use part of the loan to pay off the balance of your note. You can receive cash in a lump sum, as a series of monthly payments or as a line of credit* you draw upon as needed. The amount of the reverse mortgage loan you can get depends upon several factors: your age, current interest rates, the plan you choose and the value of your home. The older you are, the more money a lender will give you because they foresee a shorter period of time before they get their money back. Loans are available from both federally-insured and private lenders.

Of course, as with anything else, there is a downside. You will pay fees, just as with any other loan. There are caps on the amount you can get, no matter how valuable your home. If you fail to make your property tax payments, maintain homeowner's insurance or keep your house in good repair, the bank can foreclose on the loan. Your home must continue to be your primary residence. If you move out—to assisted living, for example—the deal is off. When your home is sold or upon your death, the loan must be repaid. This is a non-recourse loan, which means the lender cannot go after any other assets if for some reason the proceeds from the sale are not enough to cover the debt. If there is any excess equity, it goes to you or your heirs.

Reverse mortgages can be a valuable income-producing tool in your retirement plan, but there are many considerations before you sign on the dotted line. Laws vary from state to state, so it is important you get advice specific to your situation. AARP is a good resource for general information about these loans. See www.aarp.org/revmort for some unbiased information.

A Final Word on the Subject

Most financial advisors are in universal agreement on one thing: "old age" is not the time to bet the farm on high-risk investments. You simply do not have the time to recover from a major loss. But exactly what age is old? I have known and read about many people in

---

* Lines of credit are not allowed in every state.

INVESTING STARTING FROM SCRATCH

their fifties and beyond who have taken huge chances. Some left lucrative careers and others cashed in their life savings to start whole new lives. Whether it was a new career, a new business venture, sailing around the world or taking a volunteer post in Zimbabwe, they had something in common: they listened to their hearts and followed their dreams. Some have been profoundly successful and others only marginally—but then again, how do you measure that? Success is another ambiguous term each of us must define in our own way. Perhaps you are a kindred spirit and you are struggling with decisions about your next move. You may be asking yourself, "How much do I want this? How confident am I that I can pull it off?" and "Is there a plan B?"

> To dare is to lose one's footing momentarily. To not dare is to lose oneself.
> —SOREN KIERKEGAARD

Sometimes changes are forced upon us because of an unexpected life event, like a layoff or a divorce. You can view it as a tragedy or you can see it as an opportunity to chart a new course. We don't get do-overs in life, either, so we have to make this one count. Live it for all it's worth.

THE BOTTOM LINE

- As a rule of thumb, many financial advisors advocate withdrawing no more than four percent annually from your portfolio to minimize the risk of outliving your assets.
- Your individual tax situation will determine which baskets to sell from first, but usually it is from the taxable accounts.
- The IRS requires you to begin taking distributions from traditional IRAs beginning at age seventy and one-half. The minimum amount is based on your life expectancy.
- Annuities are contracts sold by insurance companies that are designed to pay you an income stream for the rest of your life or for a specified time period.
- Annuities are either fixed, variable or equity-indexed; and they can be deferred or immediate.
- The option you select to receive the benefit of an annuity will determine the amount and duration of your payments and there are multiple variations of these.

Selling Your Eggs

- Probably the biggest criticism of annuities by financial professionals is the tax rate on withdrawals.
- A reverse mortgage is a loan against the value of your home you do not have to repay as long as you live there.
- The amount of the reverse mortgage loan you can get depends upon your age, current interest rates, the plan you choose, and the value of your home.
- Reverse mortgages are governed by the laws of your state, so it is important to seek qualified advisors before considering this product.

> **Dream as if you'll live forever, live as if you'll die today.**
> —JAMES DEAN

"You saved $126 for your retirement. My advice is to convert it all to pennies and reinvest it at the nearest wishing well."

CHAPTER TWELVE

When You Don't Have Enough Eggs: A Plan for the Grasshoppers

Every financial advice book you read tells you to start filling your basket early, but what if you haven't? First, don't beat yourself up over this. Simply decide you are going to take some action starting today and take comfort in the fact you are not alone—many of us have procrastinated planning for retirement. An article in an AARP *Bulletin*, ("Color Me Confident" by Paul Magnusson, July/August, 2006) notes these gloomy statistics:

- Thirty-one percent of workers age forty and older have not saved a dime. Many said that lack of financial discipline was a contributing factor.
- Forty-five percent of working age households are at risk of being unable to maintain their pre-retirement standard of living.
- Forty-eight percent of people who describe themselves as confident about having enough money to live on have not tried to calculate their retirement savings needs.
- Fifty-eight percent of retirees report Social Security is a major source of their income.
- More than half of workers see their current level of debt as a problem.

Bummer. Ready for some good news? The same article quoted Alicia H. Munnell, the Director of the Center for Retirement Research at Boston College, as saying "Even relatively modest adjustments—working two extra years or saving three percent more—can substantially improve retirement security." We know what we *didn't* do; now let's look at what we *can* do.

> The past is the past, unless you still owe for it.
> —Jon Hanson

Get Out of Debt

"Buy now, pay later" is an idea that has taken firm root in our domestic soil. Americans owe more than people in any other country in the world. In fact, our debt load has tripled since 1990, and household debt burdens are at near-record highs. Bankruptcies and foreclosures are rampant. If you are drowning in debt, you are definitely not alone. Getting out of debt is your first priority.

Start by Assessing Your Situation

You know there have to be some changes made, but where to start? Today, right now, this minute, resolve not to dig the hole any deeper. Promise yourself not to buy anything on credit. Take the cards out of your wallet and put them in an inaccessible place. I knew one woman who placed her credit cards in a water-filled plastic bag and then put it in the freezer—now that's pretty inaccessible.

Next, you need to plug the holes in your bucket by figuring out where you spend money. For the next thirty days, record every penny you spend—not an estimate and not at the end of the day, but as you go. Carry a little notebook and a pen and record your purchases as you make them. Don't do anything differently than you normally do—except not charging. You are not budgeting; you are merely observing your spending behavior. At the end of each week, categorize your expenses and total them. Categories should include such things as groceries, utilities, entertainment, eating out, transportation, clothing—you get the idea. You can decide on your own categories, but make them meaningful. If you lump everything under "miscella-

When You Don't Have Enough Eggs: A Plan for the Grasshoppers

neous" you won't be any better off than where you started. At the end of the fourth week, total your spending by category for the month and *voila*! You now have the answer to "Where does it all go?" Since you have resolved not to use credit, you should not have more going out than coming in, which already puts you a step ahead.

Create a Plan

Take a close look at where your money went. Is there some fat to be trimmed? Some reprioritizing that needs to be done? Take some time to think this through and then put your budget in writing. Now make a list of all your debts, including mortgages, car loans, student loans, and credit cards. Next to each item, record the total due, the monthly payment, the minimum payment, the interest rate, and the terms. How much do you have in your budget each month to pay toward this debt? If your answer is zero, is there more in your budget plan that can be cut? Some things you can sell? Additional sources of income? Brainstorm every possible solution to find the funds. Now you have moved into the driver's seat.

> Financial independence requires nothing more than having more money come in than goes out.
>
> —ERNIE J. ZELINSKI

Pay Yourself First

As strange as it may sound, when you feel like you owe everybody and their dogs, you must always pay yourself first. Retirement savings should be your number one priority. Make it a goal to put ten percent of each paycheck into your 401(k), 403(b) or whatever investment vehicle is available to you, with the vow to increase that percentage as soon as you are able. Make it automatic, preferably deducted before you ever get your check. Neglect this at your own peril. You can borrow for many things, but no one is going to loan you money to fund your retirement lifestyle. Paying yourself first also includes Uncle Sam. Contrary to popular belief, it is not a great thing to get a huge tax refund. When that happens, it means you have loaned your money, interest-free, to the government for an entire year. Make your best estimate of how much income tax you will owe, then calculate how much to withhold from your check to pay it—no more, no less.

INVESTING STARTING FROM SCRATCH

Don't Forget Your Contingency Fund

Many people live paycheck to paycheck, but living without an adequate emergency fund is like standing in the open door of an airplane without a parachute. Any life-changing situation—such as an unexpected lay-off, an illness, accident, or a divorce—can become the crisis that throws you over the edge. Make it a goal to save ten to twelve percent every month by cutting expenses on everyday items. Writer David Bach refers to this as your "latté factor" in his book, *Smart Women Finish Rich*.

> A jug fills drop by drop.
> —BUDDHA

Pay Off Your Debts, But Pay the Right Debts First

Credit card debt is almost always the most costly and should usually be tackled first. *Sometimes* it makes sense to pay it down before you contribute to your emergency savings fund. I know this contradicts what I just said in the preceding section, but there is not a one-size-fits-all solution. Becoming debt free is the goal and there is more than one path to the destination. For example, it does not make sense to pay fifteen percent or more in credit card interest while you are earning single-digit interest on your savings. If you pay your credit cards off, you open up available credit that you could draw upon in an emergency. Of course, this assumes you have stopped using them. Widening the gap between what you owe on your credit cards and your credit limit improves your credit score. If you have to get a loan you may be able to get better rates. As soon as the cards are paid off, you can start contributing to your emergency fund.

Dealing with Your Creditors

It is a mistake to try to avoid dealing with your creditors. Owing money does not make you a pariah. Jerrold Mundis sums it up nicely in his book, *How to Get out of Debt, Stay Out of Debt and Live Prosperously* when he writes, "What you are is one of two parties in a simple business transaction. You both want the same thing: you want the money to be repaid. All that is under discussion is the best way to do that."

Don't wait until they call you. Call them first and explain your sit-

When You Don't Have Enough Eggs: A Plan for the Grasshoppers

uation as honestly and forthrightly as you can. Tell them you want to pay your debt and how you plan to do it. I know this is difficult and they may or may not be responsive, but do it anyway. Keep a record of every phone contact and copies of all letters and e-mails. Stay in control. Remember no one can make you pay more than you can pay and you now know exactly what that amount is. What matters here is your good faith effort and you may be pleasantly surprised at the response you receive.

> In earlier times, having too much debt was a crime. Debtors' prisons weren't outlawed in the U.S. until 1841.

I grew up in a family who owned a small business. I clearly recall an elderly woman who purchased something on credit and then fell on hard times. She called us and told us about her situation, that she intended to pay her bill and could send us $5 per month. She made her payments like clockwork. Impressed by her integrity and determination, we waived further interest and, at one point, offered to write off the debt, but she politely refused. We celebrated with her when the bill was finally paid in full. She emerged from the situation with her dignity and her credit intact. Here are some suggestions to try when dealing with your creditors:

Credit Card Issuers
- Call your credit card company and ask for a better rate.
- Transfer your balances to a lower-rate card, but do not max it out.
- Pay off the card with the highest interest rate first, or
- Pay off the card with the balance that is closest to its limit.
- Decide which account to pay off first and focus on it. Pay the minimums on all the others. Keep doing this until you have reached that lovely number—zero. Have a little celebration, and then start on the next one. One caveat: Some cards invoke penalty rates when you consistently pay only the minimum due. Call your credit card issuers and ask them if they have that policy. If the answer is yes, add a little extra to your payment.

> Credit card companies make huge profits from interest. The credit card industry term for people who pay their balances in full each month, depriving them of profits from interest and finance charges, is "deadbeats."

Mortgage Lenders

Many people think banks and mortgage lenders cannot wait to take their properties, but this is simply untrue. Lenders do not want your house. They are in the business of making loans, not selling foreclosed properties. They have stockholders and investors who most assuredly do not like to see unsuccessful loans on their books. They are motivated to help you find solutions.

- Talk to your lenders. Be honest about your situation. If your distress is temporary, they may grant a forbearance for a few months and allow you to pay interest only. Make sure you talk to someone in the loss mitigation department and not the collections department.
- If you need the monthly payments reduced, ask if the lender can restructure the loan to extend the term. You will pay more in the long run, but you will not lose your house. When things improve, you can double up on payments.
- If your house is simply unaffordable, it may be better to sell it. Sometimes the lenders will allow you to make interest-only loans until the property is sold, or you may be able to secure an interim loan from a friend or family member.
- If you do not have any equity in your house, selling it may not be an option. If you can't make the payments, see if you can negotiate a *short sale* with your mortgage company. In a short sale, you find a buyer, (often an investor looking for a bargain finds you) and the lender agrees to accept the proceeds of the sale as payment in full. Try to secure the lender's agreement not to report this to the credit bureaus in exchange for not having to go through the hassle of foreclosure.
- If all else fails, you can simply turn your home over to the bank or mortgage company rather than make them foreclose. This will hurt your credit, so at least try to secure their agreement not to report.

When your outgo exceeds your income, your upkeep will be your downfall.
—Walter Slezak

Auto Lenders
- Investigate the possibility of refinancing. This is a long shot, but may work if interest rates have dropped significantly since you bought the car.
- Talk to your lender about increasing your term. This will increase the amount you pay for the car, but is preferable to a repossession.
- If you are upside-down on a car, which means you owe more on the loan than the car is worth, investigate GAP insurance. This is guaranteed auto protection that covers the difference between what you owe and what the car is worth in case your car is stolen or totaled. You definitely don't want to be making payments on a car you can't afford and can't even drive. Often you can add this coverage to your regular auto policy.
- If none of this works, do your best to keep the car until it is paid off. This is known as "driving out" of the loan.

Student Loans

Student loan lenders offer a wide array of options and are about the most flexible and consumer-friendly creditors out there—unless you default. Do not ignore your loans or your lenders. Instead, try these ideas:

- See if you can have the loan forgiven. Some programs exist to either eliminate or subsidize student loans in exchange for work services. An example is teaching in an area where there are shortages of qualified personnel. See more options on www.FinancialAid.com.
- Consider consolidating your student loans and extending the terms. Shop around for the best deal.
- Defer payments on your loans if you are desperate, or ask if you can make interest-only payments. Make sure you talk to your lender—don't just stop making payments.
- Many lenders will accept partial payments or graduated payments.

The IRS

Income tax is a debt you cannot ignore, but when you can't pay it all, you may be able to set up a payment plan or negotiate a settlement with the IRS. There will be a fee for installment payments, but it is minimal. You should file your tax return on time even if you can't afford to pay—the IRS imposes a hefty penalty for failure to file. If you owe less than $25,000, you can attach Form 9465—Installment Agreement Request—to your tax return to set up a plan. You can choose the terms and payment dates, but you must pay off the debt within three years. Payments can be made through payroll deduction or automatic debits from your checking account. For more information and downloadable forms, log on www.irs.gov/taxtopics, then select "Tax Payment Options," or call the IRS at 1-800-829-1040.

All of the above assumes you have paid your taxes on time in the past. If you have serious tax issues or multiple delinquencies, it can be a sticky wicket, so you will probably want to get some help from a professional such as a tax attorney.

Medical Providers

Medical expenses often hit you when you are already down, and bills can be as difficult to decipher as a doctor's handwriting. Here are some things to keep in mind:

- You have the right to detailed copies of your bills. Check them for accuracy and dispute any errors.
- If you have health insurance, pay attention to what your insurer does and does not pay and stay after them like a bloodhound on the trail if they have rejected a claim for an expense that should be covered. With insurance companies, the squeaky wheel truly does get the grease.
- Talk to the doctor or hospital about your alternatives. Often they will agree to installment payment plans. They can also waive penalties or reduce the amount due in exchange for a lump-sum settlement.

Dealing with Collection Agencies

If your account has been turned over to a collection agency, here are some things you need to know:

- By law, a collection agency has to abide by certain guidelines.

When You Don't Have Enough Eggs: A Plan for the Grasshoppers

For example, they cannot call you at odd hours (early morning or late at night), use obscene or threatening language, or call you at your job if you have told them not to. They cannot call you repeatedly. They cannot tell others about your debt or threaten you with actions they are barred from taking.
- A collection agency is supposed to follow up the initial phone call with a written notice detailing what you owe and how to dispute it.
- You can negotiate with collectors. The best tactic is to offer a lump sum settlement. Never agree to automatic bank drafts to settle your debts.
- Keep good records and make sure you get any agreements in writing.

Last-Ditch Efforts

When you have tried your best to negotiate and nothing is working, you may want to consider hiring an attorney to negotiate with your creditors. Ask for local referrals or check the National Association of Consumer Advocates website at www.naca.net for a complete list of attorneys who specialize in this.

Non-profit credit counseling is an option, but using these services as mediators with your creditors can have a negative effect on your credit report. If you decide to go this route, check out the agency first. Make sure it is affiliated with the National Foundation for Credit Counseling (www.nfcc.org). It is much better to create your own repayment plan instead.

When the Situation is Beyond Redemption

We all want to pay our debts, but life is not painted in black and white and there are circumstances when that is just not possible, no matter how much we try. Companies that employ people with very specialized skills shut down or have layoffs. Deaths and divorces rip our safety nets apart, and medical bills can be a crushing burden even to the most prepared of us. Life happens. Filing for bankruptcy does not carry the stigma it once did. Although the bankruptcy does remain on your credit report for up to ten years, people who get their financial houses in order can restore their credit scores to near prime status within about four years of filing. Bankruptcy should, of course, be a last option—but it is an option.

"Unless we receive the outstanding balance within ten days, we will have no choice but to destroy your credit rating, ruin your reputation, and make you wish you were never born. If you have already sent the seven cents, please disregard this notice."

When You Don't Have Enough Eggs: A Plan for the Grasshoppers

Don't Kill the Hens That Lay the Golden Eggs

Borrowing from your 401(k) is a bad idea. I know borrowing from yourself seems like a good idea, but here are six reasons why that thinking is flawed:

> Do NOT borrow from your 401(k) except in the direst of circumstances—like, you need a brain transplant.

1. Most plans will not allow you to make contributions until your loan is repaid. That means you are not saving, which is the whole point of having the account in the first place.
2. You are missing out on tax-deferred returns from investments, not only on the money you have withdrawn, but also on the money you cannot contribute.
3. You are losing valuable time. It is very unlikely your balance will reach the level it could have if all your money had been working for you.
4. If you cannot repay the loan, it will be treated as a distribution subject to taxes and an early withdrawal penalty.
5. Most loans require immediate repayment if you quit your job. This means you are stuck at your job until you repay your loan—unless you treat it as a distribution and pay the taxes and penalty.
6. It delays facing the fact you are probably living beyond your means.

> Funds already spoken for must remain silent when opportunity knocks.
> —Jon Hanson

Some Final Dos and Don'ts

Do:
- This bears repeating: Communicate with your lenders.
- Get copies of your credit reports and check them for errors. Correct any you find. There are three major credit bureaus and you are entitled to one free credit report a year. You can order your report at www.AnnualCreditReport.com.

Investing Starting from Scratch

- Pay your bills on time—always. Late payments are credit killers.
- Keep a wide gap between your credit limit and what you owe.
- Always read the fine print. If an offer looks too good to be true ... you know the rest.

Don't:
- Take out consolidation loans. The fees are usually astronomical and you end up paying more than you would if you just paid off your debts.
- Pay a fee to companies offering debt elimination services. Some are outright frauds. If they are legitimate, the settlements they negotiate wreak havoc on your credit score.
- Take out a home equity loan to pay off credit card debt. Unless you change your ways, you will just be turning short-term debt into long-term debt. In addition, you are replacing unsecured debt (credit cards) that could be wiped out in a bankruptcy with secured debt (your home) that will stay with you.
- Cancel your credit cards as you pay them off. This actually hurts your scores. Sounds ironic, but you have to have credit to get good credit scores.
- Accept balance transfer offers on new credit cards unless you can pay off the balance before the low rate expires. Read the fine print.

Avoid Like the Plague:
- Payday loans. These shops seem to be springing up like mushrooms—the poisonous variety. The price you pay for that little tide-over until payday? An annualized interest rate of up to 650%.
- "Pink-slip" loans are loans secured by the value of your car. If you do not repay, the lender simply takes your car. These loans have annualized interest rates of almost 300%.
- Advances against direct deposits. If your paycheck is directly deposited to your checking account, your helpful bank may offer you the "convenience" of borrowing against your next check. The price of this is way too high.
- Tax refund anticipation loans. Instant refunds sound good;

When You Don't Have Enough Eggs: A Plan for the Grasshoppers

why wait for the government to process your tax return? Because it costs you up to 200%, that's why.
- Pawnshop loans. Sell your item in the classifieds or on eBay instead.
- Rent-to-own deals. Save your money first—then buy. It will cut the price by more than two-thirds.

> **Never spend your money before you have it.**
> —THOMAS JEFFERSON

CHAPTER THIRTEEN

Staying in Control of Expenses

STAYING IN CONTROL OF YOUR EXPENSES simply requires that you save more and spend less. This requires large measures of determination and discipline, a pinch of creativity and a dash of imagination. I highly recommend regular brainstorming sessions—even if you are the only participant in the process—to generate ideas. Here are some of my cost-cutting ideas to get you started, beginning with the necessities:

> The time to save is now. When a dog gets a bone, he doesn't go out and make a down payment on a bigger bone. He buries the one he's got.
> —Will Rogers

Housing

- If you are just buying a home, the rule of thumb is that housing costs should not exceed twenty-five percent of your gross income.
- After all your other debts have been paid off, make extra principal payments on your mortgage. You do not need to use the lenders "special plan" to do this (there are usually fees attached). Simply send in more than the regular payment, making sure you designate it as additional principal. Paying even one extra payment per year can reduce your total significantly. An easy way to do this is to make half your normal monthly payment every two weeks. Here's an example: Suppose you have a mortgage loan of $100,000 at an interest rate of 6.25% and a term of thirty years. By making bi-weekly payments,

your loan will be paid off almost six years early and you would save more than $27,000 in interest. That's not chicken feed! Why should you wait until all your other debts are paid off? Because mortgage debt is almost always the least expensive debt we owe, and if it is at a fixed rate, it gets cheaper as time passes due to inflation.

- As soon as you can, cancel your PMI (Private Mortgage Insurance) if it is included in your loan. Lenders require PMI from borrowers who put less than twenty percent down on their home loans. When your mortgage balance reaches eighty percent or less of your home's original purchase price, and if you have a good payment history, you can drop this added expense.
- Keep an eye on interest rates. If rates drop significantly from your mortgage interest rate, consider refinancing. Make sure it's worth it, because you will have to pay closing costs again on a new loan.
- Learn to make as many home repairs yourself as you can and attend to them quickly. Putting off repairs and routine maintenance chores can be costly.
- Is downsizing an option for you? If so, consider moving to a less expensive area or into a less expensive house. Check out "Great Places to Retire" on www.RetirementLiving.com or www.BestPlaces.net to compare cost of living among cities around the country. You can search for a home in all areas of the United States on www.Realtor.com, or you can subscribe to local newspapers in areas you are interested in. An interesting site for a different type of house is www.notsobighouse.com.

Food

- Go meatless a minimum of one night per week. The more, the better—for your budget, the planet, and your waistline.
- Expand your soup recipe collection.
- Pack your lunch. No matter how cheap fast food is, it is an expense to your health none of us can afford.

Staying in Control of Expenses

- Don't overbuy at the grocery store. Make a list, stick to it, and avoid shopping when you are hungry.
- Eat more fruits and veggies. Not only will you save at the market, you will save on medical bills.
- Buy fresh, buy seasonal, and buy local whenever you can.
- Want to cut your food bill in half? I can tell you how in three little words: *Cook at home.* Your bank account will gain and you will lose (pounds). A bonus is your health will probably improve, too.
- Think you don't have time to cook? Dust off the slow cooker.
- Another timesaver is to make enough for multiple dinners during one session in the kitchen. For example, baked chicken tonight, chicken spaghetti another. Planning menus in advance makes it easy to prepare a shopping list, and you don't have to make decisions about what to prepare at the end of the day when you are tired.
- Try the store brands. Goods are often made with the same ingredients—frequently by the same manufacturer—as the more expensive brands and are usually cheaper, even if you use coupons.

Transportation

I have a relative whose sole requirement for a car is that it must "start from the seat." For the record, he has not owned a car in years—he's been too busy traveling the world using the money he saves. I, on the other hand, live in an area where public transportation is non-existent, so a car is a necessity. Here are some ways to keep the costly little beasts under control:

- Reject the idea of cars as status symbols; they are transportation. Where are those gorgeous mountain roads you see in car commercials anyway?
- Keep it simple. The more bells and whistles you have on your car, the more things to maintain and repair.
- Keep your car well maintained. Change your oil frequently (about every 3,000 to 5,000 miles) as well as your air filter.

Have your tires rotated at the same time. Keep fluid levels where they are supposed to be, and follow the recommended maintenance guidelines for your model.
- Plan to keep your car for a long time. I kept my last one for thirteen years. It did not have power anything, and I never had to make a major repair.
- When you finish paying off your current ride, keep making payments—to yourself. Deposit them each month into an interest-bearing account. The next time you have to buy a car, pay cash.
- Don't use premium gasoline unless your manufacturer specifically recommends it.
- Walk and bike more, drive less. Do this enough and you can cancel that health club membership, too.
- When you have to drive, plan your errands in logical clumps.
- Check insurance rates *before* you buy a car.
- Increase your insurance deductible to the highest you can afford. This is what your contingency fund is for.
- Leasing a car is generally a bad idea. You have to pay maintenance on a car that is not yours. You pay a penalty for mileage that goes over your allotted limit, and if you decide to buy the car at the end of the lease term, you will usually end up paying more than if you had just financed it in the first place.
- Wash your car at home. It will be cleaner and you'll get a little exercise as well.

Clothing

- Don't buy anything that has to be dry-cleaned unless you absolutely, positively, can't do without it.
- Buy clothes at the end-of-season sales.
- Shop resale stores.
- Trade with friends.
- Concentrate on quality. Cheap clothes are no bargain.
- Buy classic styles with an eye toward mixing and matching with what is already in your closet.

Staying in Control of Expenses

- Reconnaissance shop. Go in with a definite idea in mind of what you want and the price you want to pay. Get in, find it (or not) and get out.

Everything Else

- Avoid catalog shopping. You tend to buy things you don't really need. Better yet, don't even look at catalogs.
- Don't subscribe to magazines. Publishers make a lot of money selling mailing lists and that's where a lot those catalogs come from. Read magazines at the library, instead.
- Follow the "Cool Rule" for luxury purchases. If you see something you really want, wait a day or two to buy it. If you still want it—and it doesn't put you further in debt—then go ahead. Often you'll find you've lost interest.
- Use coupons.
- Use your library. It is a wonderful resource, and it's absolutely free.
- Take advantage of reduced prices when they are offered, such as afternoon matinees or off-peak tee times.
- Travel during the off-season for your destination. Not only will you save money on airfare and hotels, you will also find smaller crowds and get better service.
- Try a vacation at home—no work allowed.
- Save Starbucks for special occasions—like date nights with your significant other or time out with friends.
- Use cash. It is psychologically more difficult to part with cash than to hand over the debit card.
- If you share funds with a significant other, decide together how to handle larger purchases. Establish a stop limit. Amounts over that limit require discussion and joint approval before the purchase is made. Not only does this reduce impulse buys, it maintains harmony.
- Keep track of your spending. You will be amazed how much can slip through your fingers on things you really don't need.

> Never itch for anything you aren't ready to scratch for.
> —Ivern Ball

INVESTING STARTING FROM SCRATCH

- Don't pay for services you can do yourself.
- Skip the extended warranties offered by the store on appliances and electronics. Your chances of using the insurance are small—but the cost is not.
- Be energy efficient. Close doors, turn off lights, turn up thermostats, and only run full loads of clothes and dishes. Good for you and for the environment, too.
- Entertain more at home. Potluck parties are fun.
- Shop for the best deals on everything—phone, cable, insurance, electricity—any of the necessities. Opt out of add-on services you will never use. How many channels can you watch?
- Ask for generic drugs when you get a prescription from your doctor. If there is no generic, check the cost before you fill the prescription. Often there are cheaper alternatives that will work just as well.
- Decide, in advance, how much you can afford to spend on holiday gifts. Remember the rarest gift of all in our busy world is the gift of your time and undivided attention. I recommend giving it freely.
- Make going out to dinner a special occasion. Have drinks and appetizers at home first. Enjoy them slowly and you may never leave the house.
- Increase the deductibles on your homeowners and auto insurance policies to the maximum you can afford.
- Review your life insurance policies. Do they still make sense in your current situation?

> The cost of a thing is the amount of what I will call life which is required to be exchanged for it, immediately or in the long run.
> —HENRY DAVID THOREAU

- Think quality, not quantity. Buy things that will last.
- Instead of buying an expensive specialty item, consider some alternatives. Can you rent it? Borrow it? Barter for it? Split the

cost with others? Hire the job done? Do a cost/benefit analysis first, especially if it is an item that will be used infrequently.
- Don't buy two (of anything) when one will do.
- Simplify your life. Get rid of the smoothie-makers, the bread machine, the panini press and all the other stuff collecting dust. If you don't use it, enjoy looking at it, or it doesn't have great sentimental value, get rid of it. Sell it, donate it, recycle it, or trash it.
- Before you make any purchase, consider the cost in "life units." Calculate how much your time is worth per hour, then ask yourself, "If I worked × number of hours and someone handed me this item in exchange, would I consider it a fair trade?" This puts values into perspective.

A Special Note for Those with Children

Do you know what your kids really want? Your time and attention. Think back on your own best childhood memories. Are you remembering the things you were given? Or did the fun times you had with your family come to mind first?

- If you want to teach your kids to value things more, give them less.
- If you celebrate Christmas, have your child choose the one thing that is her heart's desire. If possible, give her that. Throw in some stocking stuffers if you want, but Christmas Day at your house should not look like the local Toys R Us.
- Let your kids experience the joy of giving. Have them select an outgrown toy to give to charity before receiving anything new.
- Teach your kids the joy of pay-as-you-go. Teach them budgeting, banking and investing. Then they won't be reading books like this when they are adults—they'll be sailing in Fiji instead.

Work is Not a Four-Letter Word

If you have completed your financial worksheets and find retirement is not an option for you, please do not be discouraged, because

Staying in Control of Expenses

you are not alone. The new trend among Baby Boomers is not about retirement—it is about reinventing ourselves. Because we are living longer and staying healthier well beyond the age that used to be considered old, we have been given the gift of experimenting with second, third or even fourth careers. Some gerontologists refer to our extended life spans as the "second half" of life; others call them bonus years.

In 2005, Merrill Lynch conducted a study about retirement that surveyed more than three thousand Baby Boomers. Results revealed the vast majority of Boomers have no interest in a retirement based on leisure—only seventeen percent of the respondents planned to stop working completely. Some said they planned to work part-time or start their own businesses, but the most popular concept for the ideal lifestyle was cyclical retirement. Many Boomers plan to cycle in and out of the workforce for the rest of their lives, with intermittent periods devoted to education and leisure.

Think you are too old to go back to school? Think again. Study after study proves you *can* teach an old dog new tricks. Older students do not process new information the same way as younger students, but once the lessons are learned, they are deeply embedded. Think when you are "old" you can no longer be active? Try telling that to former President George Bush, who made parachute jumps to celebrate both his seventy-fifth and eightieth birthdays. Even if you are not up to that much of a challenge, physical capabilities are no longer an impediment to finding satisfying employment. Today, there are job opportunities that did not exist even a decade ago with many more on the horizon. The internet has spawned countless cottage industries, and the U.S. Government estimates that by 2025 (or sooner), eighty-five percent of the jobs in our economy will be in the service sector.

When we began our working lives, many of us drifted into fields that might not have been our first choice, but we stayed because we had obligations and needed the money. Now that your priorities are in order and your spending is under control, you may find a way to tailor your lifestyle so that you can do what you love. Circumstances might have dictated our first vocation, but the next one can be selected with care and thought, filtered through our wisdom and life experiences. One of the benefits of aging is that we allow ourselves to be more who we are and are less interested in impressing others.

Investing Starting from Scratch

The place to start your search for your second half vocation is within. It is not uncommon for our dreams to be buried under so much debris from our daily lives that we have lost touch with them. Take time for reflection and ask yourself questions such as the ones that follow. You are looking for your core passions; if you need help, get input from others who know you well.

1. Make a list of jobs you've had in your life. What parts of each did you like the most? What parts did you dislike?
2. Who do you like spending time with? What do you like to do?
3. Do you belong to any clubs? Volunteer organizations? What do you like about being a part of them?
4. What did you dream about being when you were a kid? Is any of it still relevant?
5. List the accomplishments in your life to date that are significant to you. Which ones have given you the highest sense of satisfaction?
6. Think of times when you felt fully alive. What made those times so special?
7. Is there something you love to do? A skill you have developed that gives you pleasure?
8. What common threads can you see in your answers?

Baby Boomers have had an impact on society every step of the way, and their older years may be more revolutionary than any other stage of their lives. Age is not something to fear—it can be the best time of your life if you embrace the opportunities presented by these bonus years. People who spend their days doing what they like do not think of "work" as a four-letter word. It is time to be true to yourself.

> **Content makes poor men rich; discontentment makes rich men poor.**
> —Benjamin Franklin

A Reality Check

Like barkers on a carnival midway, advertisers are beckoning you to "Buy! Buy! Buy!" everywhere you turn. With the advent of the in-

Staying in Control of Expenses

ternet, you don't even have to leave home to shop—you can spend money right in the comfort of your home just by pushing a few buttons. Consider these familiar refrains:

- This season's "must have" accessory.
- No money down!
- No credit? No problem!
- Buy now, pay later.
- You deserve it (whatever it is).
- Send no money now!
- No membership fee.
- You have been pre-approved.
- Only 10 easy payments.
- Act now! This offer won't last long.
- No payments for a full year!
- And on and on ad nauseam.

In my counseling practice, I have had people tell me they would like to spend more time with their families, work at a different job, or take more time for pursuits that are more meaningful—if only they could afford to. They tell me they *have* to keep doing what they are doing—that's what they believe. What I believe is they don't want to make the necessary lifestyle changes that will enable them to do what they say they really want to do. They haven't realized they have choices in how they spend their time and money. If you remember nothing else from this book, I hope you hold on to this one idea:

> **The road to financial freedom and peace of mind is based on knowing the difference between what you want and what you need.**

Take a look at your own life. Is a large house with TVs and computers in every room and one or two late-model cars in the driveway on your "needs" list? Are your closets filled with designer clothes and shoes? How about those health club memberships, ballet classes, karate lessons and all the other activities we run our kids to? Are they on your "needs" list, too? It may be time to reevaluate.

Please don't let Madison Avenue decide how you should live your life. Create your own vision. Get to know yourself and then be yourself. Be grateful for everyday pleasures and don't take a single day for granted. Plan for tomorrow, but live for today. Maybe we weren't that far off in the '60s after all.

> The one great secret of investment success is that there is no secret. My judgment and my long experience have persuaded me that complex investment strategies are, finally, doomed to failure. Investment success, it turns out, lies in simplicity as basic as the virtues of thrift, independence of thought, financial discipline, realistic expectations, and common sense.
>
> —JOHN C. BOGLE

Epilogue

If It Is to Be . . .

Research shows many Americans are unprepared for their own retirement and have unrealistic ideas about how much they will need and how long they may live.

> Now is always the most difficult time to invest.
> —Author Unknown

Now that you have read this book, have you learned everything you need to know? No. But I hope you have learned more about yourself—your needs and desires, your tolerance for risk and how to get started on an investment plan. Can you now consider yourself a competent investor? Again the answer is no. But you have learned what questions to ask and how to find the wolf in sheep's clothing among those who would help you guard your hens.

You will often find in your reading that each proponent says his or her way is "the only safe way." I say the only safe way is to educate yourself as much as possible and make your own decisions. The media's onslaught on Baby Boomers will intensify in the coming years as marketers direct their efforts towards capturing a share of the enormous wealth of this generation. If you keep your perspective and remember that this is *advertising*—not insight or sound advice—you will be well ahead of the crowd.

There is no single right way. Not only can no one can predict the future (Wouldn't that make investing easy?), things change over time—economics, world events, politics. The optimum mix of investments is some for growth, some for income, and some for safety. Investing is about finding the right balance between risk and reward for your situation and temperament. Investing is not a get-rich-quick scheme and it is not gambling. Allowing someone else to make financial decisions for you without your participation—*that's* gambling.

The goal of this book has been to give you the tools you need to decide what makes the most sense to you. This is your race. Use all the coaches and trainers you want at the starting line, but you are going to be the one that determines how you cross the finish line. You have the tools to build with—what you do with them is up to you.

> **If it is to be, it is up to me.**

The purpose of life, after all, is to live it, to taste experience to the utmost, to reach out eagerly and without fear for newer and richer experiences.

—Eleanor Roosevelt

Appendix I: Worksheets

Worksheet 1: Determining Your Net Worth

ASSETS

Financial	Current Value
Cash	$
Checking account balance	$
Savings account balance	$
Cash value of life insurance	$
Retirement account balance(s) (IRA, 401K, 403B, etc)	$
Stocks, Bonds, Mutual Funds	$
Other asset	$
Other asset	$

Non-Financial	Current Value
Home	
Car(s)	
Furniture	
Jewelry	
Art	
Antiques	
Other	
Total Assets	$

LIABILITIES

Home loan balance	$
Car loan(s) balance	$
Student loan balance	$
Credit card(s) balance	$
Other debts or loans	$
Total Liabilities	$

(Subtract total liabilities from total assets):

Net Worth	$

Worksheet 2: Annual Expenses

Housing	Monthly	Yearly
Mortgage or rent		
Electricity		
Gas		
Water		
Repairs and Maintenance		
Other		
Subtotal		
Transportation		
Car payment		
Fares		
Fuel		
Repairs		
Other		
Subtotal		
Insurance		
Homeowners		
Auto		
Health		
Life		
Other		
Subtotal		
Food		
Groceries		
Dining out		
Other		
Subtotal		
Personal		
Medical		
Clothes		
Laundry		
Memberships		
Haircuts/Personal		
Other		
Subtotal		

Appendix I

ENTERTAINMENT	Monthly	Yearly
Movies/Videos		
Cable		
Concerts/Events		
Books/Music		
Other		
Subtotal		
LOANS		
Student		
Credit card		
Other		
Subtotal		
TAXES		
Federal		
State		
Local		
Property		
Other		
Subtotal		
GIFTS		
Friends/Family		
Charity		
Other		
Subtotal		
PROFESSIONAL		
Dues		
Attorney		
Other (C.P.A.)		
Subtotal		
SAVINGS		
Retirement		
Investment		
Other		
Subtotal		
TOTALS		

Worksheet 3: Anticipated Retirement Income

Source:	$
Pension	$
Social Security	$
	$
	$
	$
Total annual income expected	$

Appendix I

Worksheet 4: Finding Your Number

MINIMUM NEEDS PROJECTION:

Col. A	Col. B	Col. C	Col. D	Col. E	Col. F	Col. G	Col. H
Income Needed	Projected Retirement Income	Annual Portfolio Withdrawal	Portfolio Required	Current Portfolio	Increase Needed	Future $ W/D in Future $	Total Portfolio in Future $

DREAM PROJECTION:

Col. A	Col. B	Col. C	Col. D	Col. E	Col. F	Col. G	Col. H
Income Needed	Projected Retirement Income	Annual Portfolio Withdrawal	Portfolio Required	Current Portfolio	Increase Needed	Future $ W/D in Future $	Total Portfolio in Future $

Appendix II: References and Resources

General Investing Books

1001 Financial Words You Need to Know, by David Bach
25 Myths You've Got to Avoid if You Want to Manage Your Money Right: The New Rules for Financial Success, by Jonathan Clements
The Armchair Millionaire, by Lewis Schiff and Douglas Gerlach
The Bogleheads' Guide to Investing, by Taylor Larimore, Mel Lindauer and Michael LeBoeuf
Boomer or Bust, by Steve Weisman
The Coffeehouse Investor, by Bill Schultheis
Dictionary of Finance and Investment Terms, by John Downes and Jordan Elliot Goodman
Die Broke, by Stephen M. Pollan
The Future for Investors: Why the Tried and True Triumph Over the Bold and the New, by Jeremy J. Siegel
The Lazy Person's Guide to Investing, by Paul B. Farrell, J.D., Ph.D.
The Motley Fool: You Have More Than You Think, by David and Tom Gardner
The Procrastinator's Guide to Financial Security: How Anyone Over 40 Can Still Build a Strong Portfolio—and Retire Comfortably! by David F. Teitelbaum
Rational Investing in Irrational Times, by Larry E. Swedroe
Smart Women Finish Rich, by David Bach
The Ultimate Safe Money Guide: How Everyone 50 and Over Can Protect, Save, and Grow Their Money, by Martin D. Weiss, Ph.D.
The Wall Street Journal Guide to Understanding Money and Investing, by Kenneth B. Morris and Virginia B. Morris

Appendix II

Chapter 2
All About Asset Allocation, by Richard A. Ferri, CFA
Buckets of Money. How to Retire in Comfort and Safety, by Raymond J. Lucia, CFP
Live it Up without Outliving Your Money!: 10 Steps to a Perfect Retirement Portfolio, by Paul Merriman
The Number, by Lee Eisenberg
The Savage Number, by Terry Savage
Understanding Asset Allocation, by Scott Frush
You're Fifty, Now What? Investing for the Second Half of Your Life, by Charles Schwab

Chapter 3
All About DRIPs and DSPs, by George C. Fisher
The Intelligent Investor, by Benjamin Graham
The Motley Fool Investment Guide, by David and Tom Gardner
One Up on Wall Street, by Peter Lynch
The Only Investment Guide You'll Ever Need, by Andrew Tobias
Take Stock, by Ellis Traub

Chapter 4
All About Bonds and Bond Mutual Funds, by Esme Farber
The Money-Making Guide to Bonds, by Hildy Richelson and Stan Richelson

Chapter 6
Investing in REITs, by Ralph L. Block

Chapter 7
All About Index Funds, by Richard A. Ferri, CFA
Common Sense on Mutual Funds: New Imperatives for the Intelligent Investor, by John C. Bogle

Chapter 8
All About Hedge Funds, by Robert A. Jaeger
Futures 101, by Richard Waldron
Hot Commodities, by Jim Rogers
How the Future Markets Work, by Jake Bernstein

Chapter 9
Parlay Your IRA into a Family Fortune, by Ed Slott

INVESTING STARTING FROM SCRATCH

Chapter 11
Die Broke, by Stephen M. Pollan and Mark Levine
Don't Die Broke, by Margaret A. Malaspina
Parlay Your IRA into a Family Fortune, by Ed Slott
Pocket Idiot's Guide to Annuities, by Ken Little
Yes, You Can Still Retire Comfortably! by Ben Stein and Phil DeMuth
You're Retired, Now What? Money Skills for a Comfortable Retirement, by Ronald M. Yolles, JD, CFA and Murray Yolles, JD, MBA

Chapter 12
The Automatic Millionaire: A Powerful One-Step Plan to Live and Finish Rich, by David Bach
Deal with Your Debt: The Right Way to Manage Your Bill$ and Pay Off What You Owe, by Liz Pulliam Weston
Good Debt, Bad Debt: Knowing the Difference Can Save Your Financial Life, by Jon Hanson
How to Get Out of Debt, Stay Out of Debt and Live Prosperously, by Jerrold Mundis

Chapter 13
Get a Life: You don't need a Million to Retire Well, by Ralph Warner
How to Retire Happy, Wild and Free: Retirement wisdom that you won't get from your financial advisor, by Ernie J. Zelinski.
The New Retirement. The Ultimate Guide to the Rest of Your Life, by Jan Cullinane and Cathy Fitzgerald
Retire on Less Than You Think, by Fred Brock
The Simple Living Guide, by Janet Luhrs
Simplify Your Life: 100 Ways to Slow Down and Enjoy the Things That Really Matter, by Elaine St. James
Your Money or Your Life-Transforming Your Relationship with Money and Achieving Financial Independence, by Joe Dominguez and Vicki Robin

Helpful Websites
www.aarp.org/bulletin/yourmoney tools for calculating debt reduction, amount needed in retirement, asset allocation and more
www.investopedia.com for good explanations of investment options
www.navanet.org: Good resource for information about annuities
www.investorwords.com for a comprehensive glossary
www.practicalmoneyskills.com for a good retirement calculator
www.tomorrowsmoney.org for calculators, tutorials, and more

Glossary

12B-1 Fees Fees charged by mutual funds to pay distribution expenses and advertising costs.

401(k) A qualified investment plan offered through an employer.

403(b) A qualified investment plan offered through an employer for employees of certain tax-exempt organizations such as churches, colleges, libraries and some non-profit institutions.

AAMS Accredited Asset Management Specialist

APR Annual percentage rate or the annual rate of interest paid without taking compounding into account.

APY Annual percentage yield or the annual rate of return that takes the effect of compounding interest into account.

accrual bonds A type of bond where all the interest earned accumulates and is not paid out until the bond matures or comes due.

Advance Health Care Directive A document that designates your wishes for medical care or treatment if you should become unable to give your own consent. Also known as a Living Will.

annuity A contract issued by an insurance company that guarantees periodic payments for a designated time in return for a premium payment. Premiums may be paid over time or in a lump sum. Annuities may be fixed, variable, or equity-indexed.

appreciate (asset) An increase in value of an asset over time.

asset An item of economic value; something you own.

asset classes Different types of investments categorized into groups. The big four are stocks, bonds, cash, and real estate.

asset-backed bond Bonds that represent shares in pools of debt such as credit cards, auto loans, and accounts receivable.

balance sheet Part of a company's financial statement showing the company's net worth at any given point in time.

INVESTING STARTING FROM SCRATCH

banker's acceptance   A short-term credit instrument guaranteed by a bank and usually used to fund international trade.

barbell technique   A technique used to distribute risk evenly over a period of time by buying half short-term and half long-term debt instruments.

bear market   When market prices are generally headed down and investor sentiment is negative.

Blue chip stock   Mature, large-cap companies with steady levels of sales and a proven track record.

bond unit investment trusts   A selection of bonds held in a fixed portfolio until the last one matures.

bull market   Periods of optimism when market prices are generally headed up and investor sentiment is positive.

buying on margin   A high-risk strategy that uses borrowed money to purchase securities.

call provision   A debt instrument that contains a call provision gives the issuer the right to pay it off before the stated maturity date.

capital   Wealth; most often refers to cash.

capital gain (or loss)   An accounting term for the difference between the buying price and the selling price of an asset.

certificate of deposit   A savings certificate that typically entitles the investor to receive a fixed rate of interest at the end of a specified term.

CFA   Chartered Financial Analyst

CFP   Certified Financial Planner

CFS   Certified Fund Specialist

CFTC   The Commodity Futures Trading Commission

ChFC   Chartered Financial Consultant

CLU   Certified Life Underwriter

commercial paper   A type of unsecured promissory note issued by large corporations, utilities, finance companies and other industries.

common stock   A security that indicates a share of ownership in a company. A common stockholder has a claim to part of the company's assets and earnings.

compound interest   Interest earned on the principal (initial investment) and on the reinvested earnings.

convertible bonds   Bonds that can be converted into common stock at a pre-set conversion ratio.

corporate bonds   Debt instruments issued by a corporation as a way to raise funds for operations. Often long-term.

corporate retail notes   Medium-term, fixed-rate, unsecured debt instruments in $1,000 increments. Usually issued by large, highly rated corporations

Glossary

cost basis The price paid for each share or unit of an investment.
coupon rate The interest rate paid by a bond.
CPA Certified Public Accountant
CRPC Chartered Retirement Planning Counselor
current yield The return a bond earns annually expressed as a percentage of the investment.
debenture A debt instrument that is not secured by any specific assets.
debt instrument A document representing a loan made for a pre-determined length of time at a pre-determined rate of interest.
defined benefit plan A retirement plan offered by an employer that guarantees a certain payment upon retirement, either in a lump sum or in the form of pension income. The amount of the payout is usually based on length of service.
defined contribution plan A retirement plan offered by an employer such as a 401(k) or 403(b) to which the employee contributes. The employer may or may not make supplemental contributions. The employee assumes responsibility for investment decisions.
deflation Economic condition in which consumer prices decrease.
depreciation (of an asset) A decrease in value of an asset over time.
derivative A type of investment that derives its value from another asset. The most common derivatives are futures contracts and options.
DESP Direct Enrollment Stock Purchase Plan
DIP Direct Investment Plan
dividends The portion of the company's net profit that is divided among stockholders. Dividends must be declared by the company's board of directors.
DRIP Dividend Reinvestment Plan
DSPP Direct Stock Purchase Plan
Durable Power of Attorney A document that gives legal authority to another person to make financial and legal decisions for you if you should become incapable of managing your own affairs.
earnings multiple Another term for price to earnings (P/E) ratio.
Efficient Market Hypothesis A theory that states it is impossible to beat the market consistently without unacceptably high risks.
equity The difference between the market value of real estate and the amount owed a lender.
equity-indexed annuity A fixed annuity with the added feature of additional earnings from stock market returns based on changes in a selected index such as the S&P 500.
eurodollars American dollars deposited at banks located outside the United States, often as a result of international trade.

exchange-traded funds Funds of securities that (usually) track an index but trade like individual stocks. Funds can hold not only stocks and bonds, but commodities and precious metals as well.

Fallen Angels Bonds that were once investment grade but were downgraded when the issuing company's financial condition deteriorated.

FFO Funds from operations. Used to measure the performance of a REIT.

FINRA Financial Industry Regulatory Authority

fixed annuity The premium paid by the investor earns a rate of interest guaranteed by the insurance company. Periodic payment amounts are also guaranteed.

fixed income investments A type of investment that provides a predetermined (fixed) return, usually in the form of interest payments.

fixed rate bonds Bonds with a set interest rate for the life of the bond.

floating rate bonds Bonds which have interest rates that are reset at predetermined time intervals. Interest rate changes are aligned with a benchmark such as the Treasury bill rate or the prime interest rate. Also known as variable-rate bonds.

FOREX The Foreign Exchange Market. A virtual market where all currencies of the world are traded.

fundamental analysis A method used to analyze stock for purchase that focuses on the intrinsic value of a company.

futures Contracts agreeing to buy a fixed amount of an asset for a set price on a specific date in the future and traded on a futures exchange.

general obligation bond A type of municipal bond issued for public works and repaid by tax revenues.

government agency bonds Bonds issued by major federally owned or federally sponsored agencies. The most common are mortgage-backed securities.

growth investors A stock selection strategy that focuses on the earnings of companies.

hedge fund Usually formed as a limited partnership by high net-worth investors. Hedge funds are not regulated by the SEC, which means managers are free to use higher risk strategies such as leverage, selling short and hedging with derivatives.

high yield bonds Bonds issued by companies with low (or no) credit ratings which pay a higher rate of interest to attract investors. More commonly known as junk bonds.

income investors An investment selection strategy that focuses on obtaining current income in the form of dividends, interest or other payments.

Glossary

index (stock) A statistical measure that tracks market trends using a selected portfolio of stocks.

index fund A mutual fund that attempts to mirror the performance of a particular stock index.

inflation The rate at which prices in the economy are rising.

IPO Initial Public Offering. The first sale of newly issued stock shares to the public.

investing Putting capital (cash) into something (such as securities) with the expectation of making a return.

IRA Individual Retirement Account. Available through a variety of custodians, all subject to IRS rules and regulations.

Jumbo CD Certificates of deposit that generally have minimums of $100,000.

junk bonds Bonds issued by companies with low (or no) credit ratings which pay a higher rate of interest to attract investors. Also known as high yield bonds.

laddering A technique used with fixed income investments to help minimize interest rate risk.

large-cap stock Companies with market caps over $10 billion.

liability A debt; something you owe.

Living Will A document that designates your wishes for medical care or treatment if you should become unable to give your own consent. More formally called an Advanced Health Care Directive.

loads The commission paid to the broker or salesperson for the purchase of shares of a mutual fund.

market capitalization The total value of all outstanding (owned or on the market for sale) shares of a company. This is commonly referred to as market cap.

market order An order to buy or sell a stock at the current market price.

MER Management Expense Ratio. Information about ongoing mutual fund management fees found in the fund's prospectus.

mid-cap stock Companies with market caps from $2 billion to $10 billion.

Modern Portfolio Theory Theory developed by economist Harry Markowitz that asserts a combination of well-researched investments of different types in a portfolio reduces the risk of loss.

money market account A savings account with higher minimum balance requirements that pays higher rates of interest than a regular savings account. Offered by most banks and credit unions.

Monte Carlo Modeling A sophisticated computer program that uses a large number of variables to design an individual investment plan.

mortgage-backed securities   Asset-backed securities with claims to pools of cash generated by payments of mortgage loans.
moving averages   The average of a security's price over a specified period of time.
municipal bonds   Bonds issued by municipalities such as cities, states, counties, school districts, airport districts and hospital districts to fund public works.
mutual fund   A basket of securities owned by a pool of investor capital. A fund may contain stocks, bonds, cash instruments or some combination of these.
net asset value   The total of a mutual fund's assets minus its liabilities. Commonly referred to as NAV.
net worth   An individual's total assets minus total liabilities.
no load funds   Mutual funds that do not charge commissions or sales fees to purchasers.
non-qualified plans   Savings plans funded with after-tax dollars so there are no limits on maximum contributions.
offering memorandum   The document that outlines the investment objectives of a hedge fund.
option   A type of derivative that conveys the right—but not the obligation—to buy or sell the underlying asset.
over-the-counter (OTC) market   A virtual market where securities are traded electronically through communications networks.
par value   The face value of a security.
pass-through securities   A frequent reference to mortgage-backed securities because the lenders withhold a small fee before passing the homeowners' payments on to investors.
PEG ratio   A ratio used in fundamental analysis. It is the P/E ratio of a stock divided by the annual growth of earnings per share.
penny stock   Highly speculative issues of companies that are sold outside of the stock exchanges.
pip   The smallest move the price can make between the bid price and the ask price in currency trading.
PMI   Private Mortgage Insurance. Usually required by lenders for borrowers who put less than twenty percent down on their home loans.
portfolio   The term used to describe an investor's total savings and investments.
Power of Attorney for Health Care   A legal document that designates a person to give—or withhold—consent for medical treatment if you are unable to do so.
preferred stock   A separate class of stock issued with different rules that

Glossary

vary from company to company. Generally, preferred stockholders receive dividends and have a higher claim on assets than common stockholders have in the event a company fails.

price multiple Another term for price to earnings (P/E) ratio.

price to earnings (P/E) ratio A ratio used in fundamental analysis to determine the value of a stock. It is calculated by dividing the market value (price) of a stock by its annual earnings per share. Also referred to as price multiple or earnings multiple.

principal The original amount of an investment.

prospectus The legal document that contains the rules and regulations for a mutual fund as well as its investment objectives.

put bond A bond that contains a provision that allows the bondholder to cash in a bond before it matures for the face value plus the interest earned to that point.

qualified plan A retirement plan that is funded with pre-tax dollars and subject to the rules of the IRS regarding retirement accounts.

rate of return The value of an investment at the beginning of a period of time compared to the value of the investment at the end of that period expressed as a percentage.

RBD Required beginning date. The day when you must begin taking required minimum distributions from your IRA per IRS regulations.

REIT Real Estate Investment Trust

repurchase agreement A very short-term loan where the borrower uses securities, usually T-bills, as collateral for a loan with the agreement the borrower will buy the securities back again later for a specific price.

revenue bonds A type of municipal bond issued to raise funds to build specific projects such as toll roads and athletic stadiums. These bonds are repaid by the income earned from the people who use the roads and facilities.

reverse mortgage A loan against the value of your home that you do not have to repay as long as you live there.

reverse stock split When a company decreases the number of existing shares. A one-for-two reverse split means an investor who owned two shares now owns one, which effectively doubles the price for the remaining share.

Rising Stars Junk bonds that are improving with the issuing company's credit rating. These may eventually become investment quality.

RMD Required Minimum Distribution from an IRA determined by the regulations of the IRS.

Roth IRA An individual retirement plan funded by after-tax dollars. All earnings in a Roth are exempt from taxes and there is no mandatory withdrawal age. Income limitations apply.

Rule of 72 A quick method to calculate out how long it will take to double an investment when it compounds at a particular rate of annual interest.

SEC Securities and Exchange Commission. A federal regulatory agency that functions to monitor the securities industry to protect investors.

sector A stock classification tool that designates a group of companies in the same industry.

secured bonds Bonds backed by collateral such as company equipment or financial assets.

security An investment instrument representing ownership that has value and can be bought and sold.

SEP Simplified Employee Pension. A type of IRA available for use by small employers or people who are self-employed.

short selling A hedging strategy where an investor sells borrowed shares of stock because she believes she will be able to rebuy them later at a lower price.

simple interest The money earned only on an initial investment or principal.

SIPC Securities Investor Protection Corporation, a non-profit corporation funded by its member broker-dealers that is designed to protect investors if a brokerage becomes insolvent.

small-cap stock Companies with market caps from $300 million to $2 billion.

speculator A person who invests in higher risk investments in the anticipation of a higher return. More often referred to as traders.

split rating (bonds) The result when bond rating agencies do not agree on the soundness of a company.

stock split Occurs when a company increases its number of stock shares even though the total value of the shares remains unchanged. This is often done to make share prices more attractive to investors.

street name Shares of stock held in the name of the brokerage to facilitate electronic transferring of shares. The investor is listed as the beneficial owner.

technical analysis A method used to buy and sell stock that focuses on the movements of the market itself rather than on the values of individual companies.

time draft A financial draft with a specific, pre-determined payment date.

TIPS Treasury Inflation-Protected Securities. A type of treasury security

Glossary

designed to protect against inflation by providing a guaranteed return over and above the inflation rate.

tracking error The difference between the performance of an index fund and its benchmark.

Treasury Bills Debt instruments issued by the U.S. treasury that mature in one year or less. Commonly referred to as T-Bills.

Treasury Bonds Debt instruments issued by the U.S. treasury that mature more than ten years after purchase.

Treasury Notes Debt instruments issued by the U.S. treasury that mature in one to ten years.

triple net lease A lease in which the tenant pays for repairs, utilities and insurance in addition to the rent.

unsecured bonds Bonds that are not backed by collateral. The issuer simply promises to pay the debt at maturity.

value investors A stock selection strategy that looks for stocks that are underpriced in relation to their performance and long-term fundamentals. Value investors believe the market overreacts to good and bad news, causing stock prices to get out of sync with reality.

variable annuity An annuity purchased with one or more premium payments that are invested in one of the insurance company's investment subaccounts. Subaccounts are similar to mutual funds and may be composed of stocks, bonds, or other securities. Returns from variable annuities fluctuate with the market depending on the underlying investment performance, which means payout amounts will not always be the same.

yield The return earned on a bond investment, expressed as a percentage. There are different types of yield, but one of the most important is yield-to-maturity.

yield-to-maturity The percent an investor will earn annually if the bond is held until it matures and all interest is reinvested at that same rate of return.

zero coupon bonds A type of accrual bond. No interest payments means no coupons.

Citations

Page 11, Norman R. Augustine in the *Harvard Business Review*, "Managing the Crisis You Tried to Prevent," Nov/Dec, 1995, Vol. 73 Issue 6.

Page 12, Herb Greenberg in "Herb on The Street" from *The Street* (3/4/98).

Page 20, Jerrold Mundis from *How to Get Out of Debt, Stay Out of Debt & Live Prosperously*. Copyright 1988. Published by Bantam Books. Reprinted with permission.

Page 24, Mark Skousen at the Las Vegas Money Show (6/7/99).

Page 32 and **36**, Peter Lynch from *One Up on Wall Street: How to Use What You Already Know to Make Money in the Market*, by Peter Lynch with John Rothchild. Copyright 1989. Published by Simon and Schuster. Reprinted with permission.

Page 39, Jeremy Siegel, quoted by James M. Pethokoukis in "Consulting the Oracles," *US News & World Report*, Vol. 123, Issue 18, p. 34 (11/10/97).

Page 51, Larry E. Swedroe from *The Only Guide to a Winning Bond Strategy You'll Ever Need: The Way Smart Money Preserves Wealth Today*, by Larry E. Swedroe and Joseph H. Hempen. Copyright 2006. Published by Truman Talley Books, St. Martin's Press. Reprinted with permission.

Page 86, Ralph L. Block from *Investing in REITs*, by Ralph L. Block. Copyright 2006. Published by Bloomberg Press. Reprinted with permission.

Page 101, From *Step Right Up* by Tom Waits.

Page 102, Burton Malkiel in *Global Bargain Hunting: The Investor's Guide to Profits in Emerging Markets*, by Burton Malkiel and J. P. Mei. Copyright 1999. Published by Simon & Schuster, Inc. Reprinted with the permission of Simon & Schuster, Inc.

Page 104, style box reprinted by permission of Morningstar, Inc.

Page 106, Paul Samuelson from *Bloomberg* (September 1999).

Page 107, John Brennan in "Lessons Learned From 2000" from *Mutual Funds Magazine* (January 2001).

Page 117, Werner De Bondt at the Association for Investment Management and Research Annual Conference (5/25/99).

Page 130, Jim McTague in "The Advice Game" from *Barron's* (8/4/97). Reprinted with permission.

Page 136, Jonathon Clements in *25 Myths You've Got to Avoid—If You Want to*

Manage Your Money Right: The New Rules for Financial Success by Jonathan Clements. Copyright 1998. Reprinted with the permission of Simon & Schuster, Inc.

Page 150, George Foreman from "Tuning Up for Ali" by Bill Rhoden in *Ebony Magazine*, March 1976.

Page 151, Dave Barry from *Dave Barry Talks Back* by Dave Barry. Copyright 1991. Published by Three Rivers Press. Reprinted with permission.

Page 152, Jonathan Clements from "Playing the Right Retirement Cards" in the *Wall St. Journal* – Eastern Edition, 11/16/99, Vol. 234, Issue 97.

Page 164 and **page 173**, Jon Hanson from *Good Debt, Bad Debt* by Jon Hanson. Copyright 2005. Published by Penguin Group. Reprinted with permission.

Page 165, Ernie J. Zelinski from *The Joy of Not Working: A Book for the Retired, Unemployed and Overworked—21st Century Edition* by Ernie J. Zelinski. Copyright 2003. Published by Ten Speed Press. Reprinted with permission.

Page 188, John C. Bogle from his speech at the Money Show, Feb. 3, 1999, "The Clash of the Cultures in Investing: Complexity vs. Simplicity."

Index

AAMS, 131, 201
accrual bonds, 49, 56, 201, 209
Advance Health Care Directive. See *Living Will.*
American Assn. of Individual Investors, 37
American Stock Exchange, 31
annual percentage rate (APR), 3, 72, 76, 201
annual percentage yield (APY), 72, 76, 201
annuity, 134, 152-158, 160, 201, 203, 204, 209
appreciate (asset), 2, 84, 85, 158, 201
asset, 1, 2, 7, 9, 18, 32, 33, 43, 51, 61, 73, 79, 81, 85, 92, 96, 102, 103, 110, 114-118, 121, 125, 134, 137, 143, 145, 151, 155-160, 193, 201
asset allocation, 22, 26, 95, 96, 104, 107, 199, 200
asset classes, 6, 9, 47, 84, 92, 95, 201
asset-backed bonds, 63

balance sheet, 85, 131, 201
balanced fund, 95
banker's acceptance, 8, 74, 202
barbell technique, 66, 202
base currency, 123
bear market, 6, 40, 41, 45, 67, 202
Better Investing, 36
blend funds, 94
Blue Chip, 33, 39, 94, 97, 202
bond unit investment trusts, 64, 202
Bretton Woods Agreement, 122

bull market, 6, 40, 44, 65, 202
buying on margin, 112, 113, 125, 202

call option, 118, 119, 121
call provision, 49, 202
call risk, 49, 66
capital, 2, 24, 32, 36, 61, 67, 91, 109, 202
capital gain (loss), 53, 80, 83, 94, 99, 100, 103, 107, 110, 140, 143, 147, 157, 202
certificate of deposit (CD), 3, 4, 6, 7, 8, 26, 70, 71, 72, 73, 76, 92, 202
CFA, 131, 132, 202
CFP, 131, 202
CFS, 131, 202
ChFC, 132, 202
Chicago Board of Trade, 115
Chicago Board Options Exchange, 118, 121
CLU, 132, 202
commercial paper, 8, 72, 73, 76, 92, 202
Commodity Futures Trading Commission, 117, 202
common stock, 32, 62, 202
compound interest, 3, 4, 76, 202
convertible bonds, 62, 202
corporate bonds, 61, 63, 66, 93,202
corporate retail notes, 61, 62, 202
cost basis, 139, 157, 203
country funds, 95
coupon rate, 48, 52, 54, 62, 203
CPA, 131, 203
cross currency, 123
CRPC, 132, 203
current yield, 50, 51, 203

213

custodian, 55, 136, 137, 152, 205
cyclical retirement, 185

debenture, 61, 203
debt instrument, 7, 58, 69, 92, 202, 203, 209
debt securities, 3, 8, 67
default risk, 48, 66
deferred annuity, 134
defined benefit plan, xxiii, 133, 203
defined contribution plan, xxiii, 133, 203
deflation, 54, 203
depreciation, 2, 85, 89, 203
derivative, 110, 115, 118, 125, 203, 204, 206
DESP, 43, 203
DIP, 43, 44, 46, 203
dividend, 32-35, 39, 43, 46, 79, 80, 83, 84, 88, 89, 94, 99, 103, 107, 114, 140, 203, 204, 207
Dow Jones Industrial Average, 97
DRIP, 43, 44, 46, 88, 199, 203
DSPP, 43, 203
Durable Power of Attorney, 146, 147, 203

earnings multiple, 36, 203, 207
effect of declining interest rate on bonds, 52
effect of increasing interest rate on bonds, 53
Efficient Market Hypothesis, 97, 203
equity, 2, 9, 18, 158, 159, 168, 174, 203
equity investments, 3, 9, 40, 77, 93, 104
equity REIT, 77, 79, 81, 87, 88, 89
equity-indexed annuity, 153, 154, 160, 201, 203
eurodollars, 74, 76, 203
exchange traded fund, 47, 88, 98, 99, 107, 204

Fallen Angels, 62, 204
Fannie Mae, 58, 59, 93
FDIC, 71, 75, 76
Federal Home Loan Bank System, 60
Federal Home Loan Mortgage Corporation, 59
FFO, 85, 89, 204

Fidelity, 23, 106
Financial Planning Association, 128
FINRA, 41, 42, 64, 72, 158, 204
Fitch, 48
fixed annuity, 153, 157, 203, 204
fixed income investment, 7, 49, 95, 204, 205
fixed rate bonds, 49, 50, 52, 204
floating rate bonds, 49, 204
foreign funds, 93, 94
FOREX, 122, 123, 124, 125, 204
Form ADV, 128
401(k), xxiii, 1, 19, 133-137, 154, 165, 173, 201, 203
403(b), xxiii, 1, 134-137, 154, 165, 201, 203
Freddie Mac, 58, 59
fundamental analysis, 36-39, 46, 124, 204, 206, 207
futures, 115-118, 121, 125, 199, 203, 204

GAP insurance, 169
general obligation bonds, 57
Ginnie Mae, 58, 59
global funds, 94
Global Industrial Classification Standard, 34
Gold Fixing, 121, 125
government agency bonds, 57, 58, 60, 204
government sponsored enterprise (GSE), 58, 61, 66
growth funds, 94, 95
growth investors, 38, 40, 46, 84, 204

hedge fund, 109, 110, 125, 199, 204, 206
hedging, 79, 110, 116, 121, 125, 204, 208
high-yield bonds, 62, 63, 66, 93, 204, 205
hybrid funds, 95

immediate annuity, 154, 155
income funds, 94
income investors, 39, 46, 84, 93, 204
index, 71, 86, 97, 98, 99, 103, 109, 115, 142, 205
index fund, 88, 97, 98, 99, 101, 105, 106, 107, 110, 143, 199, 205
Industrial Revolution, xix

Index

inflation, 8, 19, 22, 26, 35, 45, 51, 54, 56, 57, 66, 84, 86, 89, 121, 178, 205
inflation risk, 8, 54, 66
initial public offering (IPO), 32, 46, 205
interest rate risk, 54, 60, 64, 92, 205
IRA, 135, 136, 137, 151, 152, 160, 199, 205

Jumbo CD, 205
junk bonds, 48, 94, 207. *Also see high-yield bonds.*

laddering (technique), 62, 64, 65, 66, 205
large-cap, 33, 34, 94,97, 98, 202, 205
leverage, 110, 112, 113, 124, 125, 204
liability, 2, 100, 205
Life Cycle Fund, 95
Lifestyle Fund, 96
Living Will, 146, 147, 201, 205
loads (mutual funds), 64, 101, 205

Management Expense Ratio (MER), 102, 205
market capitalization, 33, 46, 205
market order, 42, 205
market risk, 43, 48, 54, 60, 66, 71
Markowitz, Harry, 24, 205
mid-cap, 33, 34, 94, 205
Modern Portfolio Theory, 24, 27, 205
money market, 7, 24, 67, 69, 75, 76
money market account, 76, 205
money market mutual fund, 74, 75, 76, 92
Monte Carlo Modeling, 22, 26, 205
Moody's, 48, 73
Morningstar, 64, 88, 103-106, 142
mortgage REIT, 79
mortgage-backed securities, 58, 59, 60, 63, 79, 93, 204, 206
moving averages, 38, 206
municipal bonds, 57, 63, 66, 93, 204, 206, 207
mutual fund, 1, 8, 47, 59, 62, 63, 66, 73-76, 88, 91-107, 110, 121, 131, 134, 135, 139, 142, 143, 145, 153, 157, 193, 199, 206
Mutual Fund Education Alliance, 106

NAREIT, 88
NASDAQ, 31, 97, 98
National Association of Consumer Advocates, 171
National Association of Personal Finanacial Advisors, 128
National Foundation for Credit Counseling, 171
net asset value (NAV), 100, 105, 107, 200, 206
net worth, 1, 2, 9, 12, 18, 85, 143, 193, 206
New York Stock Exchange, 31, 41, 47, 80
no-load funds, 102, 106, 206
non-exchange-traded REIT, 80
non-qualified plan, 154, 157, 206

offering memorandum, 110, 206
optional cash payments, 43
options, 115, 118, 119, 120, 121, 125, 203
over-the-counter market, 47, 206

par value, 51, 206
pass-through securities, 60, 206
PEG ratio, 37, 206
penny stocks, 44, 206
percentage rent increase, 86
pink slip loan, 174
pip, 124, 206
portfolio, 7, 11, 17-20, 24-29, 34-39, 41, 47, 48, 62, 64, 75, 83, 84, 88, 89, 92, 96-98, 103, 111, 128, 130, 134, 142-145, 147, 151, 160, 197, 206
Power of Attorney for Health Care, 146, 147, 206
preferred stock, 33, 206
prepayment risk, 60
price multiple, 36, 207
price to earnings (P/E) ratio, 36, 37, 203, 207
principal, 3, 4, 51, 59, 60, 71, 134, 135, 141, 157, 177, 207
private mortgage insurance (PMI), 178, 206
private REIT, 80

prospectus, 47, 72, 75, 95, 96, 100, 105, 106, 107, 207
put bond, 50, 207
put option, 120, 121
qualified plan, 133, 154, 157, 207

Quicken, 142, 143, 144, 147
quote currency, 123

rate of return, 51, 54, 57, 140, 141, 147, 207
rebalancing, 142, 145, 147
reference rate, 49
regional funds, 95
reinvestment risk, 49
REIT, 9, 77, 79-81, 83-89, 95, 151, 199, 207
repurchase agreement, 74, 76, 207
Required Beginning Date (RBD), 151, 152, 207
Required Minimum Distribution (RMD), 151, 152, 207
revenue bonds, 57, 207
reverse mortgage, 158, 159, 161, 207
reverse stock split, 40, 207
Rising Stars, 62
Roth 401(k), 133
Roth 403(b), 135
Roth IRA, 135, 152, 207
Rule of 72, 5, 8, 9, 208
Russell 2000 Index, 98

sector, 33, 34, 61, 93, 94, 142, 208
sector funds, 95
secured bonds, 51, 208
Securities and Exchange Commission (SEC), 31, 32, 64, 72, 73, 75, 76, 80, 84, 100, 110, 125, 128, 158, 208
Senior Citizens Freedom to Work Act, 150
SEP, 136, 137, 152, 208
Series EE Savings Bonds, 56, 57
Series I Savings Bonds, 56, 57
shareholder of record, 43
short sale, 168
short selling, 114, 208
simple interest, 3, 4, 208

SIPC, 43, 64, 208
small-cap, 33, 34, 38, 94, 97, 98, 105, 106, 208
Social Security, xix, xxiii, xxiv, 16, 150, 163, 196
Socially Responsible Funds, 95
speculators, 62, 116, 121, 122
split rating, 48, 208
spot market, 123
stalwarts, 35
S&P 500, 97, 98, 153
step-up basis, 157
stock exchange, 31, 32, 41, 46, 80, 99
stock split, 40, 208
street name, 42, 44, 208
strike price, 119, 120

Target Date Fund, 96
technical analysis, 37, 38, 46, 124, 125, 208
1035 Exchange, 155
1099, 83, 100
time draft, 74, 208
TIPS, 54, 56, 208
tracking error, 98, 209
Treasury bills (T-bills), 7, 8, 69, 70, 73, 74, 75, 76, 92, 209
Treasury bonds, 54, 92, 209
Treasury Direct, 55, 56, 69, 70
Treasury notes, 54, 209
triple net lease, 87, 209
12B-1 Fee, 102, 201

U.S. Government Bond Fund 92
unrealized gain (loss), 141, 147
unsecured bonds, 51, 209

value fund, 94
value investors, 38, 46, 84, 209
Vanguard, 23, 97, 106
variable annuity, 156, 158, 209
variable rate bond, 49, 204
variable rate CD, 71

Wilshire 5000 Total Market Index, 98
yield-to-maturity, 51, 64, 209
zero coupon bonds, 49, 56, 209

About the Author

Janet Holt, MS, LPC, is a gerontologist and licensed professional counselor whose mission is to help people make sense of their lives. She is also a Baby Boomer who set out to understand why everybody was making money from her retirement savings but *her*. Janet regularly speaks to groups and teaches classes on financial literacy. She also offers a continuing education seminar for other counselors about the special challenges faced by Boomers. For a current list of workshops and seminars, visit www.janetholt.com.